WRITING RELIGIOUSLY
A GUIDE TO WRITING
NONFICTION RELIGIOUS BOOKS

ABOUT THE AUTHORS

DON M. AYCOCK is a pastor, free lance writer, literary agent and doctoral candidate. Educated at Louisiana College, Southern Baptist Theological Seminary and Oxford University, and now completing the doctorate at New Orleans Baptist Theological Seminary, he has written several books and a wide variety of articles. The pastor of the Enon Baptist Church of Franklinton, La., he and his wife, Carla, have twin sons Ryan and Christopher, and reside in the New Orleans area.

LEONARD GEORGE GOSS works in religious publishing as a book editor, free lance writer, book club director, and lecturer on writing and publishing. A graduate of both Phoenix College and Arizona State University, he obtained the M.Div. from Trinity Evangelical Divinity School, Deerfield, Ill. Presently pursuing additional graduate studies at the University of Windsor, Ontario, he lives in the Detroit area with his wife, Carolyn, and their sons Joseph and David.

WRITING RELIGIOUSLY
A GUIDE TO WRITING
NONFICTION RELIGIOUS BOOKS

Don M. Aycock

and

Leonard George Goss

MOTT
MEDIA

WRITING RELIGIOUSLY: A Guide To Writing Nonfiction
Religious Books

Copyright © 1984 by Don Milton Aycock and Leonard George Goss

First Edition

Printed in the United States of America
ISBN 0-88062-117-6

To My Best Supporters and Critics:
My beautiful wife, Carla, who patiently awaited the birth of
our twins while I pampered another "child"—this book.
Joe Johnson, an editor friend in Nashville, was the first person
to actually treat me as a writer. He offered both encouragement
and an occasional kick in the rump. I needed both.

(D.M.A.)

To My Mother
Sylvia Rosenberg Goss
and
to the Memory of My Father
Joe Goss
With All Respect and Great Love

(L.G.G.)

CONTENTS

Foreword by Sherwood Eliot Wirt ix

Preface xi

Chapter 1 WRITING: The Challenge and The Process 1

Chapter 2 IDEAS: How to Get and Preserve Them 17

Chapter 3 MECHANICS: Getting It On Paper 35

Chapter 4 EDITORS: How To Contact and What
           To Send 49

Chapter 5 SUBSTANCE: What Do Editors Want? 61

Chapter 6 THE PUBLISHING CONTRACT: What Does
           It All Mean? 77

Chapter 7 TOOLS: Know What Is Available 105

Chapter 8 MARKETS: Where To Sell Your Books 125

Chapter 9 SELECTIVE BIBLIOGRAPHY: Some Of The
           Better Books On Writing and Publishing .. 161

Epilogue 177

Appendices:

           A. WRITING ARTICLES 181

           B. WRITING CURRICULUM 209

           C. A SAMPLE STYLEBOOK for Authors,
              Editors and Proofreaders in the
              Preparation of Manuscripts 221

Name Index 253

FOREWORD

For the past twenty years and more I have had the rewarding pleasure of encouraging writers to get into print. Most of these people have had their eyes set on authoring a book. Were I to hazard a guess as to the number of people in the United States who at this moment are engaged in trying to write a book, it would be in the millions. Those I have met are eager, diligent, conscientious, charming, and—for the most part— doomed to disappointment.

In discussing the making of books with aspiring writers in many parts of the world, I have often come across those with a subtle distinction that seems to make an enormous difference. They may have a brilliant "idea" and they may not; they may have a literary background and they may not; but there is an air about them. It is a professional air, an approach to the writing business that makes me realize that my advice is really not needed; they either know what they're doing or very soon will know. They approach writing as they would sheep farming or pilot training or practical nursing. Whatever their tactics of the moment, their strategy is sound. In a very short time they will be published.

These people are not usually attracted by the glamour of the literary set. They don't expect to storm the market with a best seller. As Christians they are motivated to serve the Lord—but so are the unsuccessful ones! What makes the difference is that these people are out to learn the craft from top to bottom. They subscribe to the right journals, attend the right conferences, seek out the right people, study the trends, and seek to meet the current demands of the readership. They think of themselves as professional writers.

This book by Don Aycock and Len Goss, if carefully studied, might well be the means of turning amateur writers into pros. It is carefully designed to bring the neophyte into the fraternity. It is loaded with practical suggestions and guidelines for writers, quotes scores of contemporary editors and publishers, and contains standard information that is often difficult to come by. The result is that this volume is a fine writer's resource textbook and teaching manual; but it is more than that. As you will learn on the first page, it is an intimate, often delightful reading experience. I wish you joy and Godspeed as you read—and write.

Sherwood Eliot Wirt

PREFACE

At their best, words are windows into the soul of another person—the writer. Perhaps this is why the printed word holds such a permanent place in the ranks of human achievement. What do these windows admit? Among other things, knowledge, inspiration, challenge, motivation, chiding, hope and plain fun to millions who read and the lesser number who write. Do you doubt it? Visit a book store and watch the ravenous looks in the patrons' eyes as they relish each title and devour each cover.

Public libraries in many towns all across the country have a sale each year to dispose of unneeded books and to raise money. These usually begin at 9:00 in the morning, but by 8:00 throngs have already gathered at the ropes which block off the books from the public. By 8:45 book mongers from all over the county have gathered. By 8:59 the library staff prepares to lower the ropes and run for their lives for fear of being trampled by a bibliophile in need of a cheap fix—a 10¢ paperback.

Books for many of these people are not luxuries, but absolute necessities. And they are not alone. While many fewer people read books than watch television, the book reading population seems to be growing. Many publishers are doing record volume business with no sign of slacking off. For example, the largest industry in Nashville, Tennessee is not, as you might imagine, the country music business. The largest is the religious publishing industry. There is a kind of quiet excitement to the whole thing.

The number of those writing books is increasing. One of us recently had lunch with an editor in a southern city who told him he was being driven crazy by the myriad number of people who wanted to write for him. Nothing was said at the time, but the author already knew that. He was one of those driving the editor crazy!

At the time of this writing, one of the authors has written four nonfiction books, coauthored another, and edited two others. He fully admits it—he's hooked! The other author got so hooked on books that he decided during graduate seminary to make a career of publishing! Our whole purpose for writing this book is to share our excitement on an intimate, personal basis with you, the reader. We have picked up tips, pointers, ideas, no-nos, maybes and musts about writing books along the way. We want to make these available to you. There is no *one* way to do it. But there are some generally accepted principles and methods of going about the writing of books and getting those books published. If we can help you make even a single step in your journey toward writing and publishing your book, then our purpose will be served, and our book worthwhile.

Chapter 1

WRITING: THE CHALLENGE AND THE PROCESS

WRITING: THE CHALLENGE AND THE PROCESS

Congratulations?

So you wish to write a book. We're not entirely sure whether to offer congratulations or condolences. Conservative estimates say that should your book be published, it will compete against 40,000 titles which will be published in the same year. Think of it—forty thousand! Imagine how many manuscripts are submitted to publishers which never see the light of day. It boggles the mind.

But we writers are a strange breed. You are thinking, "Yea, I know the competition is stiff, but verily, mine won't be one of the rejected manuscripts. Surely mine *will* make it." We applaud your courage, tenacity and slight craziness. (Anybody who wants to write a book is probably slightly crazy.) We have put this book together to help you realize that dream of seeing your book in print.

The Authors' Assumptions

We assume several things about you, the reader of this book. We assume first that you have something vital you want to say in the book you contemplate writing. Because yours is a nonfiction religious book (or else why would you be reading this guide?), it can help people live more fulfilled, complete lives. Not long ago, religious books were seen as "fluff books" —usually dramatic conversions, celebrities' accounts of their "faith," or over-simplified approaches to difficult problems.[1] This situation is changing. Now do not get us wrong. We are not against all stories of celebrity conversions and so forth, even those which are badly written. It is just that the reading public's tastes are changing. They are demanding the cookies be put on higher shelves, in more quality books with sounder themes to help one think through issues and find real solutions. They want material with more stuff and less fluff. You can deliver just such books to publishers ready to develop, produce and market them. The next section of this chapter expands this idea a little more.

A second assumption about you is that you want to share your vital message in a full book-length manuscript. You are willing to spend the hours of seemingly endless toil necessary for good writing. You are willing to give up watching "Dallas" and "Dynasty," Sunday afternoon football games (ouch!), and put up with comments from family and friends like, "Aw, he's *only* writing a book." We devote little space in this guide trying to pique your interest in writing. If you lack interest, then do not waste your time reading this book for inspiration.

Our third notion about you is that you know the rudiments of English grammar, spelling, syntax, and all the other bits and pieces of information your high school English teacher kept saying you would need to know someday. That some day is now. If you need to refresh yourself, as we all occasionally do, go to a local library or bookstore and read one or two good primers on grammar. Writing styles are as individual as fingerprints, but certain guidelines do exist. You need to know the basic principles.

A fourth assumption about you is that you are interested in writing a nonfiction *religious* book. If you plan to work on the great American novel, or an Erma Bombeck-like book of humor, or "Ninety-Six Ways to Cure Hangnails," or books of other distinct genres, we are afraid this book will not be of much help to you. Obviously some overlap on pertinent writing clues can be found in all books on writing. Chapters on editors and contracts, for examples, would be helpful to others, and much of the other material besides, but the real focus here is on nonfiction religious books.

Religious Books: What About Them?

The tastes and demands of a reading public change. The time was when books on religious themes were looked on with suspicion, both by many readers and by the publishing industry. More than one person has suggested that subsidy publishers (or vanity presses—you pay them to publish your book) often make money on books with religious subjects because so few in publishing will touch them. Referring to this type of publisher, one observer noted, "They offer a bland steady flow of essays that God is love, Nature is true, and in the long run, the Spirit triumphs."[2]

This was mostly true, especially years ago. But times certainly change and even general publishers have found a reading public for religious books. Today, many religious books outsell general books. We are not referring to the poorly written banal tomes in which some subsidy publishers specialize. Well-written books with vital themes in religion have proven they have a place in the publishing world. Many larger commercial houses now have religious departments as part of their publishing programs. These lines of books are extremely successful. And dozens of highly professional firms specialize in publishing religious titles.

A recent issue of the *Writer's Market* notes that the religious book field is healthier today than ten years ago. An editor at one of the religious publishing houses says, "New writers—who write well and who have something worth reading to write about—have unlimited opportunity."[3]

Sherwood E. Wirt, long-time editor of the famous *Decision* magazine, offers several resolutions for the would-be religion writer.[4] His suggestions would apply, of course, to any writer.

1. *I will not write corn—banal, sentimental, obvious stuffy tripe.*
2. *I will either seek to write imaginatively, or I will not write.*

> 3. *I will not waste my time on insignificant material.*
> 4. *I will write to change lives, if I can.*
> 5. *I will politely ignore those who would flatter me.*
> 6. *I will write in quantity but strive for quality.*
> 7. *I will thankfully give whatever glory comes to God, who alone imparts all gifts, including this gift.*

These ideas speak to improving religious books. But what are some of the common faults of book manuscripts in the religious field? Consider some of the following problems.[5]

> 1. *The manuscript is directed at no one. There is no focus, no special readership in mind.*
> 2. *The idea is out of date (or before its time).*
> 3. *There is no logical progression in the writing. Like Don Quixote, the manuscript goes in all directions at once.*
> 4. *The writing is sloppy. Unforgivable!*
> 5. *The author submits the manuscript to more than one publisher at a time without advising the publishers. (Multiple submissions are sometimes permitted, but be sure the publishers know about them.)*
> 6. *The manuscript is submitted to the wrong publisher. It would fit someone else's line, but not the publisher you sent it to. Queries help avoid this problem.*
> 7. *Footnotes and other similar material are not accurate or complete. Permissions and other necessary procedures thus become difficult or impossible.*
> 8. *The author had a faulty or inadequate concept of the market at which the book is aimed.*
> 9. *An agent is used incorrectly. Agents can be helpful but sometimes they get in the way if they are only duplicating the work of the author.*
> 10. *There is no Table of Contents.*

Knowing what to avoid while contacting publishers and editors will help you get started in the right direction. Now let us consider the actual process of writing religious books.

Writing: The Process
You have a great idea for a book. But you are asking

yourself, "How do I get started?" and "Am I really sure I can do this?" Almost all writers ask these questions, so you are in good company.

Let us consider the counsel of some well-known and widely respected authors of nonfiction religious books. If we learn from their experience we might be able to avoid some of the traps and pitfalls mentioned above.

William Barclay

One of the best known religious authors of our time was William Barclay, a Scottish Professor of Divinity. Barclay wrote scores of important books during his career as teacher and writer. The books have sold into the millions.

Barclay's philosophy of writing is deceptively obvious—"I can and do work."[6] In other words, he was willing to pay the price for writing. He quoted Collin Brooks who defined this process as follows: "The art of writing is the art of applying the seat of the pants to the seat of the chair." And he was not talking about the chair at the dinner table!

Barclay said he was influenced by his fellow Britisher, Winston Churchill. Churchill was a writer of incredible discipline. His multiple-volume history of the second world war attests to this fact. At his birthplace outside Oxford, England, Blenheim Palace, Churchill had an elaborate library and study. One can tell immediately that he took his writing seriously.

First-time authors sometimes do not take their writing seriously. But they can be assured that if they do not, no one else will. These writers are tempted to "wait for inspiration" before beginning. Perhaps they have never heard the dictum, "Good writing is 10 percent inspiration and 90 percent perspiration."

Someone once asked Churchill about inspiration, detractions, and other things which thwart an author's effort. His answer was typically pointed and slightly gruff:

> You've got to get over that. If you sit waiting for inspiration, you will sit waiting until you are an old man. Writing is like

any other job—like marching an army, for instance. If you sit down and wait until the weather is fine, you won't get far with your troops. Kick yourself; irritate yourself; but *write*; it's the only way.[7]

William Barclay learned his lesson well from his mentor. He worked hard at "applying the seat of the pants to the seat of the chair." Barclay's students well knew his work habits. Whenever he was not busy teaching classes or talking with his students about academic matters, he could be found at all times pounding on his typewriter. But, and his former students underscored this point, Barclay *always* had time for his students. As much as he worked at it, writing was not his god.

Barclay denied having any special gift for writing other than tenacity. In fact, he claimed never to have an original thought in his life. He called himself a "pipeline" or a "theological middleman." He felt he could take the large bills of theology and philosophy and break them down into small change so average persons could understand.[8] The ability to do this, however, takes great skill and talent. Because he was willing to do so, millions of people have benefited from his labor.

This brings us to a point which must be emphasized and re-emphasized—the person who wants to write must work hard. One of the authors once queried an editor about a book he wanted to do. The editor answered immediately and said he was interested. He wanted to see three chapters, but they were not ready. When the author beat around the bush about them, that editor wrote a short, never-to-be-forgotten note. It said,"The only way to learn to write is to write. Well?"

Phillip J. Gearing and Evelyn V. Brunson have written a good book entitled *Breaking Into Print*. Their advice on the process of getting the words from your mind onto paper is worth considering.

Writing demands self-discipline, so establish a daily routine that includes *at least two hours* to be applied to the material you are trying to produce. Many times you will sit down at the typewriter or with pen in hand thinking that you have nothing to put on paper today. But, as you sit in that writing attitude, you find yourself putting words of your paper, words you would have missed had you not kept to your routine.[9]

Norman Vincent Peale

Another well-known author of religious books is Norman Vincent Peale, Pastor of the Marble Collegiate Church in New York City. Like most successful authors, Peale has established a routine for his writing. We will let him tell about it in his own words.

I can do much better in the morning. I'm fresher. I can stick at it for a longer period of time, and my energies seem to be at a maximum. So, what I like to do when I'm writing a book, is to get out of bed at six o'clock, get dressed, have breakfast, and get everything out of the way so I can start working at seven o'clock.

I write in longhand. In fact, I write every single word myself with a pencil. I use plain white paper and have perhaps a couple dozen pencils lined up, all sharpened. I write with one until it is worn down and then throw it aside and write with another, and finally I pick them all up, sharpen them again, and then start wearing them down again. I sharpen them myself with an electric sharpener.

After I've written two to three thousand words I go through the penciled copy and mark it up. Sometimes it looks pretty terrible. Then, when I can't read it any more myself, because it is so marked up, I have it typed. I then go over the typed copy once; I may take out some material or put more in. The copy turns out to be fairly clean after the first typing, as a rule, because the major revision has been in the penciled work.[10]

Peale offers this advice to would-be authors:

I get manuscripts or several chapters from people who want to write books. In many cases, they just do not know how to go about it. They do not put it together properly. They do not build an orderly outline. They seem lacking in ability of getting the interest of the reader with the opening paragraphs, the attention getters and so forth.

They do not dramatize their material. You've got to make it so it attracts and holds the reader's interest. Sustained interest is a hard thing to achieve. Even the brightest person in the world can't hold to the same subject for too long a time.

Peale further advises aspiring authors to forget striving for literary effect. Say what you have to say in the simplest and most interesting way and then end. Avoid wordiness.

Dr. Peale learned his writing style by serving as a newspaper reporter before becoming a minister. He thus learned the art of working at a steady pace, putting people into his material, and being concise. Apparently he has learned his lesson well. His books have sold in the millions and have been responsible for helping countless persons live through crises and find fulfillment in their lives.

Harry Emerson Fosdick

The name Harry Emerson Fosdick is recognized by many as one of the most theologically creative ministers of the twentieth century. But Fosdick was also a prolific author, and like those already mentioned, he worked with a steady routine. He discusses the process of writing one of this books, *The Meaning of Prayer*:

> It started with a series of sermons, went on to a series of midweek discussions where I could get the questions, objections and difficulties of the people, and then in an abandoned cottage on the Maine coast, near our summer home, I sat down daily for two months at a rickety kitchen table in a bare room and wrote the book. When I sent the manuscript to the publishers, I told them that a book on prayer could not expect a large sale and that I thought two thousand copies would be adequate. I guessed wrong that time.[11]

Fosdick was a master at understatement. That book he wrote at the rickety kitchen table sold over a million copies and has been translated into seventeen languages.

Fosdick learned discipline early in his career. This discipline paid off during his many busy years as Senior Minister of the Riverside Church in New York City.

Elton Trueblood

One other author will help us understand, at least partially, the process of getting started on the right foot and of working steadily. That author is Elton Trueblood. Like the other men mentioned above, Trueblood has written extensively. Besides once serving as editor of a religious journal, Dr. Trueblood also wrote thirty-one books. Many of these are still in print.

In his autobiography, *While It Is Day*, he tells of his writing program and habits. As with the previous authors mentioned, let us allow Trueblood to speak in his own words. Who, better than a skilled writer, can describe his own work?

> In my case all is done longhand with a fountain pen, with ink that flows effortlessly. By this method I avoid the mechanics of the typewriter, and the speed of the pen seems to match the speed of my mind. Writing all morning in this fashion, I can without strain produce two thousand five hundred words. Because unbroken speed helps to create smoothness of style, I make only a minimum of corrections as I produce the first draft. Later, of course, especially after the chapters are typed, I substitute, delete, and add to my hearts content. But it is the original writing which is both exhilarating and energy-consuming![12]

Many authors like "to have written," that is, to be finished with the project, see their name in print, and to get the royalty check. Trueblood, however, enjoys the actual writing process and describes it for us.

> I should like to convey to my readers something of the joy of writing which I regularly experience. The very act of writing can be remarkably creative. When I sit down with paper in front of me, I know in general what I want to say, but I seldom know the details. As the ideas are expressed in written form, however, they begin to grow and to develop by their own inherent logic. Always I am a bit surprised by what has been written, for I have become in some sense an instrument.[13]

Trueblood indicates that he is a "morning person." He is

at his mental energy peak early in the morning. Thus he does his writing in the mornings only and uses the afternoons and evenings for editing and re-writing. This is not to say he never writes in the afternoons. As he puts it, ". . . the author who takes his profession seriously will expect to be invaded by ideas at all times. . . . The important thing, then, is never to be without pen and paper, for the ideas are as fugitive as they are precious."[14]

We must remember that Trueblood was also a busy professor at Earlham College in Richmond, Indiana at the same time he was doing most of his writing. How did he handle the responsibilities? Again, his counsel from his own words is helpful.

> A public man, though he is necessarily available at many times, must learn to hide. If he is always available, he is not worth enough when he *is* available. I once wrote a chapter in the Cincinatti Union Station, but that was itself a form of hiding because nobody knew who the man with the writing pad was. Consequently nobody approached me during five wonderful hours until the departure of the next train for Richmond. We must use the time which we have because even at best there is never enough.[15]

Consensus

When we take the experiences of William Barclay, Norman Vincent Peale, Harry Emerson Fosdick, and Elton Trueblood, add them together, and factor in their advice to new writers, what do we get?

First, if you are serious about writing, you must write. This sounds absurdly obvious, but many people miss it. The only way to get experience is to get experience.

Second, you need a quiet, private place in which to write. Not everyone has the luxury of owning a lavish private office or cabin by the beach. But almost everyone can find some space to call his or her own, at least for an hour or two. Your family will understand and, if requested, leave you alone for awhile.

Third, develop a routine that is right for *you*. You may not even be awake until noon. If so, then trying to write in the mornings will be frustrating and futile. Find what time of day or night is best for you and work creatively. Line up the tools which best suit your needs. For example, can you write better with a typewriter, or, like Peale and Trueblood, do you need to write everything in longhand? Perhaps you can do both. Most books on writing suggest the use of a typewriter because it is faster than writing with a pencil.

Fourth, be willing to revise and edit your own work. Your words are not inspired. They can be expanded, rearranged, or even deleted without the universe suffering irreparable damage.

By now you see how hard writing books can be. At the same time, you may and should see what joy writing can add to your life.

Writing For Quantity

Let us give you some statistics which might shock you, but it is to be hoped they will inspire you when you think about cranking out a book or two.[16]

Charles Hamilton, alias Frank Richards, creator of "Billy Bunter," averaged writing 80,000 words a week. This is about 320 pages per week, or sixty-four pages daily.

Georges Simenon, a Belgian writer, and creator of "Inspector Maigret" wrote a 200-page novel in eight days. From 1919 to 1973 he wrote 214 novels under his own name and 300 others under nineteen other pen names. His books, including many translations, sold 300 million copies.

John Creasey wrote 564 books in his lifetime. He once wrote two books in six and a half days.

Earle Stanley Gardner had 140 titles of his books published. Over 170 million copies sold.

Ursula Bloom published 468 full-length books from 1922 to 1972. That is an average of more than nine per year.

Walter Gibson, creator of "The Shadow," wrote 283 "Shadow" novels. He did it in seven consecutive years, writing one novel every two weeks. That equals about 120 pages each week.

Agatha Christie wrote 85 books, seventeen plays, fifteen films, and over 100 short stories.

Michael Avallone wrote 184 novels from 1953 to 1980, with 40 million copies being in print. He once finished a novel in one and a half days.

If you feel more depressed than inspired by such statistics, do not feel alone. Most writers will feel the same way until they reassess their own writing goals. We are not necessarily to produce a plethora of novels and short stories. At least some of us are concerned for nonfiction which takes research and planning, and would rather write a few titles considered good quality. Obviously not much revision and polishing can be done on a book written in a day and a half.

The purpose for giving these statistics is only to point out that you *can* write a book if you really want to. We know— the kids are crying; the phone is ringing; the boss called and wants you to come right back to the office for important work; you worked so hard lately you can hardly make it home, let alone write; Aunt Cheryl is coming for a visit . . . . The list is endless. But think about it this way. If you hone one typewritten page per day for two hundred days, then you will have a two-hundred page book. Put that way, it doesn't sound so hard, does it?

Let us close this chapter with a paraphrase of I Corinthians 13, written by Marian Brincken Forschler.[17] Put it under your pillow and read it before going to sleep.

I Corinthians 13 For Writers

Though I've taken ten years of English and six writing courses, attended every writer's conference within 200 miles, and know fifty writers and twelve editors, if I have not love, my writing will be hollow and shallow.

Though I write for five hours a day, study *Writer's Market* endlessly, and sell eighty percent of what I write, if I have not love, I am nothing.

Though I tithe my sales, donate book reviews to my church newsletter, host a critique group regularly, praise my fellow writer's work, study the Bible and books on writing diligently, and pray for God's guidance over my pen—if I have not love, it doesn't mean a thing.

Love doesn't get jealous when another writer sells to *Guideposts.*

Love doesn't show off a $3,500 check from *Reader's Digest* for a sale to "Drama in Real Life."

Love is not rude to those who only talk about writing and are too slothful to work or polish their skills.

Love is gracious when the editor loses your manuscript.

Love is not happy when a fellow writer's book fails to sell.

Love keeps on loving editors through rejections and soiled manuscripts.

Love isn't thwarted by interruptions of writing schedules, writer's block or harsh criticism.

Love doesn't get so busy writing that there isn't time for God, family and friends.

Love never fails. Whether there be knowledge of article forms and strong verbs, you'll forget to use them. Whether your manuscripts are long or short, some will be rejected. Whether you need payment or not, you won't get as much as you deserve.

And now abide faith, hope, and love—these three; but the greatest of these is genuine love that keeps on loving God, family, editors, other writers, and himself because of the miracle God performs in us.

NOTES

1. William Griffin, editorial in "Publishers' Weekly."

2. From an editorial, "Will You Pay To Have It Published?" in *The Creative Writer*, edited by Aron M. Mathieu (Cincinnati: Writer's Digest, 1961), p. 187.

3. Anne Geohegan in *1980 Writer's Market*, edited by William Brohaugh (Cincinnati: Writer's Digest Books, 1979), p. 56.

4. Sherwood Eliot Wirt, *You Can Tell The World*, with Ruth McKinney (Minneapolis: Augsburg Publishing House, 1975), p. 22.

5. This list is found in *The Religious Writer's Marketplace*, by William H. Gentz and Elaine Wright Colvin (Philadelphia: Running Press, 1980), pp. 109-110.

6. William Barclay, *William Barclay: A Spritual Autobiography* (Grand Rapids: William B. Eerdmans Publishing Co., 1975), p. 28.

7. Churchill, quoted by Barclay, p. 29.

8. Barclay, p. 31.

9. Philip H. Gearing and Evelyn V. Brunson, *Breaking Into Print* (Englewood Cliffs, N.J.: Prentice-Hall, 1977), p. 49.

10. Norman Vincent Peale, in Ralph Daigh's *Maybe You Should Write A Book* (Englewood Cliffs, N.J.: Prentice-Hall, 1977), pp. 157ff.

11. Harry Emerson Fosdick, *The Living Of These Days* (New York: Harper and Row, 1956), p. 91.

12. Elton Trueblood, *While It Is Day: An Autobiography* (New York: Harper and Row, 1974), p. 64.

13. Ibid.

14. Ibid., p. 65.

15. Ibid., p. 67.

16. These statistics were first compiled by A. "Doc" Shepherd in "The Christian's Writing and Self-Publishing Newsletter," Volume 1, Number 1, p. 4.

17. Marian Brincken Forschler in *The Religious Writer's Marketplace* (Philadelphia: Running Press, 1980), p.x. Used by permission of the author.

Chapter 2

IDEAS: HOW TO GET AND PRESERVE THEM

IDEAS: HOW TO GET AND PRESERVE THEM

Mark Twain once wrote to a friend, "Take your mind out and dance on it. It's getting all caked up." Unfortunately, that terrible malady was not limited to Twain's time. All of us get crusted up and must take the necessary time and effort to clear up our minds. Without doing so, we will be like ocean-going ships which get slowed down by the accretions of barnacles on their hulls. There, too, periodic scraping is in order.

Boredom and tedium are two barnacles of the mind which slow the flow of ideas and curtail creativity. The writer must want to clear them away so he or she can produce the best writing possible. You, the reader, want to produce a book. You may already have an idea about want you want to say. But that idea might not be at all clear and sharply focused. In this chapter we wish to assist you in getting ideas, working creatively with those ideas, and preserving them for your writing.

Use Your Imagination

To say, "use your imagination," to a writer is like saying, "Don't worry" to a neurotic. The obvious question is "Yes, but how?" Being creative and imaginative is no easy task for most of us. We are taught to think in certain patterns and forms. Education often teaches us *what* to think, but not always *how* to think. Many of us can be like racing horses, fitted with blinders to see only straight ahead. Certainly the mind can be thus fitted. What we want to do, then, is remove those blinders and loose our imaginations. We want to "uncake" them.

A correct assessment from David Campbell is that "creativity demands commitment. To change one's life even in a small way requires energy, participation, and enthusiasm. You cannot be creative while inert. You have to get involved."[1] Your first reaction might be to say, "But I don't have any creativity." But that is not so, for we all do. We use our creativity whenever we write anything. Some use the facility obviously more than others, but we all have it. The trick is to learn how to use it.

Understanding Creativity

What is the creative imagination? This question fascinates researchers and philosophers alike. We know the answer when we see it; we know a creative person when we see one. But even then, getting a handle on that elusive quality of creativity is tough. Famed psychologist, Rollo May devoted much attention to this issue in a book which no writer should be without, even religious writers. Entitled *The Courage To Create*, this celebrated book explores creativity and how to use it.[2] Here, he defines creativity as "the encounter of the intensively conscious human being with his or her world" (p. 56). The creative person's will, passion, and commitment to his or her subject is part of this encounter. While we may not be able to will creativity, May assures us that "we can *will* to give ourselves to the encounter with intensity of dedication and commitment. The deeper aspects of awareness are activated to the extent that the person is committed to the encounter" (p. 46). In other words, you are far more likely to be creative if you are absorbed by, enthralled and caught up in your writing than if you merely dabble with a topic of marginal interest.

May teaches that when persons are creative, they are representing the highest degree of emotional health. They are therefore "actualizing" themselves. The writer, for example, faces the wilderness of a blank sheet of paper. He accepts the challenge to conquer it; he throws all of himself into the task. Mind, will, imagination and reason all join forces to slay the dragon of the blank page. The writer tames chaos to make cosmos, that is, order, form and reason. May speaks of this process in his own writing.

> I prefer, therefore, to endure the chaos, to face "complexity and perplexity" as Barron puts it. Then I am impelled by this chaos to seek order, to struggle with it until I can find a deeper, underlying form. I believe I am then engaged in what MacLeish describes as a struggling with the meaninglessness and silence of the world until I can force it to mean, until I can make the silence answer and the non-being be (footnote, p. 108).

We do not suggest, in quoting May, that he wrote from any traditional religious perspective. But we are talking about imagination, a subject on which May can inform any writer. To write like this, using one's imagination, calls for more strength and determination that is popularly supposed. It requires, as May puts it, actual courage. He defines courage as "the capacity to move ahead *in spite of despair*" (p.3). He places it in context as follows:"Courage is not a virtue or value among other personal values like love and fidelity. It is the foundation that underlies and gives reality to all other virtues and personal values. Without courage our love pales into mere dependency. Without courage our fidelity becomes conformism" (p.4).

You, as a writer, must have the courage to create, to bring something significant from nothing. You must throw yourself into writing with verve and force. You must use language to express your very soul. W.H. Auden once remarked, "The poet marries the language, and out of this marriage the poem is born." Isn't this the way *all* good writing finds life?

Cultivating Imagination

The ability to use the imagination in your writing, like any other ability, can be strengthened and improved. Listed below are fifteen ideas and techniques you can use to great advantage in improving your imaginative capabilities.[3]

1. Commune with God's nature. Spend some time outdoors, even if it is only in a park during your lunch break. Watch carefully the sights, paying attention to color, texture, movement, and dimension. Listen to the cacophony of sounds. Try to feel the many things which interest you.

2. Read the best books available. Good reading always stimulates the imagination and teaches techniques for utilizing it. Do not read in only one area and certainly avoid only contemporary works. Meet the great writers face to face. Spread out and read the classics.[4]

3. Develop devout contemplation. Learn to take time simply to think about things. Set aside designated periods of each day to listen to the inner dialogue going on inside you.

4. Remember to keep within the limit of fact. Do not allow your imagination to supply factual information. We know of one graduate student who made up a scholar to corroborate his research. This is going far beyond the realm of cultivating a healthy imagination.

5. Be perceptive at all times. You will have to work on this one. Specified contemplative times are great, but if you keep your eyes and ears open you will be aware of all sorts of ideas and impressions continually flooding your senses.

6. Study suitable literature dealing with those specific subjects on which you work. The goal here is to feed the mind factual data and to suggest ideas for working with your subject. There will be times when you will subconsciously incorporate much of what you read. It will then emerge in new and different forms from your subconscious imagination. It will then be uniquely yours.

7. Take sufficient time to work through the material so it can be incorporated into your subconscious mind. Researchers who study the phenomenon of the imagination say that one must feed the mind but then allow time for "incubation" when the material matures. This may take days, or even years.

8. Have an abundance of your subject material on hand. This will save your frustration in having to hunt it down when you begin to get ideas and start to work.

9. Have a sufficiently difficult problem, one which challenges the intellect. If you are going to spend a large amount of time writing a book, shouldn't you be supremely interested in working with a challenging topic?

10. Try to remain optimistic about your subject. The imagination thrives on optimism.

11. Keep a sense of humor. This helps avoid frustration which thwarts creativity.

12. Endeavor to keep your motivation high. Without it, creative imagination will wane.

13. Be patient. Remember, you get the chicken by hatching, not smashing the egg.

14. Try to maintain your peace of mind. Your imagination cannot function well if your mind is filled with all sorts of worries. Remember Mark Twain's reflection:"I've had many troubles in my life, but most of them never happened." No words offer greater counsel against care than verses 25-34 in the sixth chapter of Matthew's gospel. Read and reread them.

15. Keep physically fit. A lazy body produces a lazy mind.

These ideas will help you begin developing your imagination. You simply *must* do it. W. MacNeile Dixon reminded us a half century ago that the human mind is not a debating hall but a picture gallery. Today's writers must hang pictures on the walls of that gallery. Imagination is the paint and creativity is the brush for our work.

The Imagination in Writing

A little poem speaks to a function of the imagination in writing:

> Biting my truant pen,
>> Beating myself for spite,
> Fool, said my muse to me,
>> Look in thy heart and write.

Our imaginations help us look into the heart. We can get inside ourselves, and, through imaginative thought, into the mind and heart of someone else. One author sketched this process of introspection as follows.

> Writing, like life itself, is a voyage of discovery. The adventure is a metaphysical one: it is a way of approaching life indirectly, of acquiring a total rather than partial view of the universe. The writer lives between the upper and lower worlds: he takes the path in order eventually to become the path himself.
>
> I began in absolute chaos and darkness, in a bog or swamp of ideas and emotions and experiences. Even now I do not consider myself a writer, in the ordinary sense of the word. I am a man telling the story of his life, a process which appears more and more inexhaustible as I go on.[5]

This chapter is about ideas. What we are saying is that our imaginations and creative interactions with ourselves and our world are the best sources of ideas for our writing. As Virginia Wolf once observed, "Odd how the creative power at once brings the whole universe to order." We, as writers, seek this wholeness, both in ourselves and in our external worlds.

The wise writer will therefore tap the energy of the creative imagination and make an ally of his subconscious mind. Stuart Cloete described the benefits of this latter task.

> The front of your mind is continually drifting about—prying into what your intentions are toward unpaid bills, and deciding whether you're hungry or not hungry, and thinking up clever little lines to answer the argument that was ended last night. Meanwhile your subconscious is slogging along trying to complete the job that your conscious mind is hindering.[6]

Playwright J. B. Priestley spoke of this as his being able to "tap a reservoir of creative energy and skill, which reservoir is really the source of all so-called inspiration."[7] To tap this reservoir, the writer must toil like a miner under a landslide, as someone put it.

You might be thinking that creative work can be done only

under "ideal" conditions, with everything approaching perfection. Listen to H.V. Morton's ideas as he described such a place.

> What a haven of rest! It is the place which women friends instantly declare the perfect spot for any writer of their acquaintance to "settle in" and produce a book. As I looked at the veranda, the eucalyptus trees and the sunlight, and as I listened, hearing only a mule going past on the road and a bird singing in the trees, I could imagine the sound of those decisive, ringing tones that have plagued many a man's souls: "What a lovely place to settle down and write—so quiet, so peaceful, nothing to distract you. . . ." And, flinging myself into the basket chair, I apostrophized the misunderstanding shade: "Madam," I said, "it has been proved time and again that the perfect place for a writer is in the hideous roar of a city, with men making a new road under his window in competition with a barrel organ, and on the mat a man writing for the rent."[8]

You will find rewards concomitant with the exercising of your imagination in writing. Some of these rewards include your gaining a new sense of creation. You also gain a new sense of freedom, along with a sense of self-worth and identity.[9] When you write creatively, you simply *know* that you have peeled the veneer off reality, studied its contents and described it for your readers.

We have been referring to the fact that creative writing is better for you, the author. It is also better for your readers, too. You can move the person reading your words when those words are imaginatively written far more than you can with pedestrian writing. Consider the two examples of writing styles given below and see which one stirs your own imagination and engages your will.

> ***Example 1:*** Everybody can agree that poverty is a blight on the American consciousness. "How," we collectively ask ourselves, "can we call ourselves a land of plenty and of caring, and yet allow people to live on such meager incomes?"
>
> This question is not unique nor is it new. As far back as the eighteenth century we can find traces of various organizations

whose *raison d'etre* was to alleviate the suffering of the unfortunate denizens of urban ghettos and rural slums.

Example 2:
What is poverty?

Let us be very specific and precise. It is of the senses.

Poverty is a smell. It is the cooking smell of old grease used and re-used, saturated into clothes and hair and rotting upholstery; the sleeping smell of beds crowded with ill-nourished bodies, and threadbare blankets soaked with odors of sickness and staleness.

Poverty is a sound. It is the sound of perpetual crying: an infant mewling, a mother mourning, an old man moaning. The sound is of shrieks in the night, noise the day long. Shuffling feet, hacking coughs, rustling vermin, insistent leaks and drips and crackings.

Poverty is a sight. It is the sight of slumped shoulders, useless hands stuffed into empty pockets, averted eyes. The scene is of land ill-used—barren, blasted, junk-strewn wasteland—or of streets that are blighted wilderness of asphalt, brick, steel, and random-blowing trash.

Poverty is a feeling—through the pores . . . on the feet. Cold so sharp it burns and heat so sweltering and oppressive it chills with a clammy sweat. The feeling of poverty is dull aches, twinges, pangs, brief satisfactions, creeping numbness. Pain.

Poverty is a taste. It is the taste of hot saliva boiling into the mouth before nausea, or dried beans and chicken gizzards and hog skins and too many starches and too few fruits. Stale bread and spoiling vegetables, cheap coffee and the sweet momentary fizz of soft drinks that allay but do not alleviate hunger pangs.

But poverty is more than the sum of its physical parts. It is not only hunger today but fear of tomorrow. Not only present chill but future freeze. Not only daily discomfort but accumulations of illness. It is fear, but fear made impotent by the enormity of today's demands and an insufficiency of energy to forestall tomorrow's defeats.[10]

Is there any doubt about which piece is the more creative and moving?

Write From Experience

We have been thinking about the imagination as a source of ideas for writing. Your own experience is also an excellent source. This does not rule out the creative use of those experiences. You might think that your experiences are not unique or in any way exciting. You have never been to Paris, do not have a Ph.D., nor have you had a life-threatening illness. Understand that these or similar situations are *not* necessary ingredients for experiential writing. What *is* necessary are unique individual experiences, and being true to those experiences.

Helen Hull believes that the universality of our common experiences makes excellent material for writing. She couched her argument as follows.

> The writer may refuse to see and to accept the limitations and the scope of his imagination. He finds his own material commonplace and thinks to escape its dullness by flights into more romantic, farther fields, taking passage on what he calls imagination. He does not trust his own experience, he does not value it; he does not know that within that experience, provided he can penetrate deeply enough, he possesses on the one hand all that he can achieve of originality in creative work, and on the other all he can know of universality.[11]

Did you catch that phrase, "He does not trust his own experience . . . ?" That is a problem many "average" writers have. We feel that if we could just do something special or travel to some exotic spot, then we could really write. But consider one more author's opinion about the uniqueness and trustworthiness of our individual experiences.

> To have learned through enthusiasms and sorrow what things are within and without the self that make for more life or less, for fruitfulness or sterility; to hold to the one and eschew the other; to seek, to persuade, to reveal, and convince; to be ready to readjust one's values at the summons of a new truth that is known and felt; to be unweary in learning to discriminate more sharply between the false and the true, the trivial and significant, in life and in men and in works; to be prepared

to take a risk for the finer and the better things,—that is perhaps all we can do. Yet somehow as I write, the words 'perhaps all we can do' seem a very meager phrase. The endeavor to be true to experience strikes me at this moment as the most precious privilege of all.[12]

"The endeavor to be true to experience"—there it is again. Experience is the key to good writing. This is true especially of religious books. Religion is as much a matter of the heart as of the head. One's total life experience is involved. Let us give you some personal examples.

Seminary students usually find little devotional material designed for the unique needs of budding theologians. One of the authors and his wife began writing prayers/poems for themselves. In them they tried to express their feelings and hopes, along with their frustrations. Even the title of the collection was chosen to reflect that experience. That title, written slightly tongue-in-cheek, is *Not Quite Heaven*.[13] Consider some of the following thoughts.

GRADES
2 Thessalonians 3:5

A "B—"?!
But it *can't* be!
  I worked so hard and studied so long.
The grader is crazy.
The professor is nuts.
But any idiot can clearly see that this is an "A" exam.
I know that I forgot to include the dates, but that's not
  important.
Did I really spell "religeous" wrong?

Sometimes I feel that I'm flunking the real test—life.
  You're a real hard grader, Lord.
  And there is never a chance for a makeup.
It's a strange fact, though: somehow we all pass.

LAUNDRY
Numbers 16:9
"It toileth not, neither doth it spin."
Read the sign on the broken washing machine.

Seems life here is many times like the laundry—
  Hot
  Wrinkled
  Waiting for a chance for a washer or dryer.
Eureka! At last!
  —darn, no change.

Decisions, decisions—do you dump out someone's clothes, or
  do you exercise patience?

Lord,
Help us love the person who uses the dryer for two hours for
  three towels. Amen.

The lesson here is that anyone can write from their personal circumstances, whatever they are. That same author got great mileage out of his studies for a Master of Theology degree. After completing the required thesis, he published it, and then compiled an anthology for publication of the materials from his thesis study.[14] Since he is a pastor, he often sees people who are apathetic about church membership and involvement. He sought literature designed to tell him how to help these people, but found very little. As a result, he called several professor friends and said, "Let's do a book together on this subject." Several long sessions of brainstorming and critiquing each other's work produced a book entitled *Apathy in the Pew: Ministering to the Uninvolved.*[15]

One more example: The coauthor once preached a series of sermons on Jesus' use of concrete items and situations to teach spiritual lessons. This was later expanded into essays and produced a book entitled *Symbols of Salvation.*[16]

Even this book is a result of our experiences in writing and publishing. We have learned a good deal about the technical side of writing, editing, and publishing: We are just using our experience as a source for our writing. If we did not trust our own experiences, we would have little to say.

Many people have an interest in trying to write a book. Call it creative impulse or whatever you like, but everyone seems to say at one time or another, "You know, I think I'd like to write something one of these days.'' How strange and even frightening the publishing business can appear to would-be authors. But one thing we have learned is that if a first-time writer can write reasonably well and has something to say which is said intelligibly, there is no reason that writer cannot be published.

Harry Emerson Fosdick has already been mentioned. He, too, drew from his experiences to produce many of his books. He said in his autobiography, "Wanting to know what I really thought about immortality, I broke up my questions into as orderly an arrangement as I could manage, and announced a series of Sunday evening sermons on the subject."[17] The result was the writing of one of his most popular books, *The Assurance of Immortality*.

Fosdick was also a well-known counselor. Those experiences, too, provided grist for his mill. "I distilled the essence of my experience in this field into my book, *On Being A Real Person*. There, with all possibility of individual identification concealed, I have told some of the stories of human need that came to my 'confessional'."[18]

Experience is certainly not a fool-proof guide, however. Again, we can use Fosdick as an example. He wrote a book, *The Challenge of the Present Crisis*, as a justification of the second world war. But he later repudiated its message, saying "I was never more sincere in my life than when I wrote it, but I was wrong."[19]

Harry Neal said he once happened to see a street meeting of the Salvation Army in New York City. He began to wonder what made these people tick. He wanted to know who they were. Neal began to interview members of the Army and to do research into their origin and goals. The result was the writing of a captivating book entitled *The Hallelujah Army*.[20]

If you keep your eyes open and your mind in gear, you will have plenty of experiences suggesting ideas for books. Using your creative imagination and personal experience are absolutely essential, but do not rule out two other equal essentials: interest and research. You may simply have a strong interest in language study, for example. That might help you master Greek and Hebrew which could help you write in the area of biblical exposition. You may enjoy getting to know famous persons, so your area might be interviewing. You can extensively research whatever area of interest you have, and become an "expert." Chapter 7 has more information about research methodology.

Preserving Ideas

Some unpublished writers wonder how to keep up with the various ideas they might get for books. If you ask ten different experienced authors you will without doubt get ten different ideas. Some authors jot everything down in notebooks. If they are weeding a garden, for instance, and an idea strikes them, they lay down the hoe and immediately record the idea. These people always carry a pen and pad. The memory is often faulty and an idea once forgotten is usually gone forever.

You must choose a method which works for you. One of the authors of this book always carries a pen and a shirt pocket-size notebook. Anything which seems unique gets recorded. He might overhear a conversation which illustrates a problem common to many people. A particularly strange or in some way unique event may occur. He might read a quotation or other thought he wants to keep. When he gets back to his study he rewrites the event, or whatever it is, on a 8½ x 11 piece of paper and files it for future reference.

Since one of us is a minister he preaches regularly. This pressure forces him to be alert for any possibilities for sermons or illustrations. In this regard he has developed a filing system which is simple and efficient. One way to file is to have a folder for every topic. For example, someone using this kind of system might have a file on "family," one on "future," and so on. This is all right, but it can get rather bulky. The author uses a central index on 3 x 5 cards. Whenever he has a newspaper clipping or anything else he wants to file, he simply goes to the file index, makes a note of the clipping under the appropriate category, and then marks a file number on the clipping and drops it in a file folder.

This filing system uses a continuous numbering system. The first folder is numbered 1-25. The contents may be twenty-five different subjects. The second folder is 26-50, and so on. The key to the system is the index box. Everything which goes into a folder is assigned a number. If, for example, you have an article on infant care, go to the folder presently in use. You might see that the last item there has the number GF 213. This indicates general file 213. Get a 3 x 5 card under the heading "BABY" and make a notation of what the article is about, and then assign it a number. Since the last item filed was 213, this new article is 214. Then write that number on the upper left corner of the article and drop it into the file.

In preparing the writing of this chapter, index cards were consulted to see what was under the topic "imagination." On the card was GF 12, GF 64, GF 72, GF 101, and several reference to books previously read on the subject. The files were pulled and the books were reexamined. A large amount of material was at hand, material which had been cross-indexed under "creativity."

This system is not by any means new. You can read about it in various books.[21] Anything is better then keeping clippings in a shoe box! This system will serve you well, and allow you to constantly expand your files with good, fresh material on many topics. On the other hand you may find this method of filing and keeping your notes organized totally inappropriate for your needs. Find whatever works for you and use it. Filing takes time, but in the long run it saves time.

Christopher Morely once wrote, "It was a good day to fly a kite. I didn't have a kite so I went out and flew my mind." That is really remarkable advice for the creative writer. Dance on your mind, fly it as a kite, unfold it on regular intervals just as skydivers do with their parachutes. Ideas will roll forth like water over Niagara.

NOTES

1. David Campbell, *Take The Road to Creativity And Get Off Your Dead End* (Niles, Ill.: Argus Communications, 1977), p. 7.

2. Rollo May, *The Courage To Create* (New York: Bantam Books, 1976) (First published in 1975 by W. W. Norton & Co.) All references are to the Bantam edition.

3. This list is adapted from Don Aycock's article, "Using Imagination In Preaching," in *Search*, Spring 1979, p. 56. Published by the Sunday School Board of the Southern Baptist Convention.

4. The mistaken preference for the more modern books is brilliantly addressed by C. S. Lewis in his "Introduction" to Sister Penelope Lawson's translation of *St. Athanasius On The Incarnation* (New York: Macmillan Publishing Co., 1981).

5. Henry Miller, quoted in *The Choice is Always Ours*, edited by Dorothy Berkley Phillips (Wheaton, Ill.: Quest Books, 1975), p. 342.

6. Stuart Cloete, quoted in *In the Minister's Workship*, by Halford E. Luccock (Nashville: Abingdon Press, 1944), p. 205.

7. Quoted in *Workshop*, p. 206.

8. Quoted in *Workship*, p. 211.

9. These three items were suggested by Robert D. Young, *Religious Imagination* (Philadelphia: Westminister Press, 1979), pp. 152ff.

10. Wilma Dykeman, *Prophet of Plenty* (Knoxville: The University of Tennessee Press, 1966), pp. 1-4.

11. Helen Hull, *The Writer's Book,* (New York: Barnes & Noble, Inc., 1956), p. 40.

12. John Middleton Murry, quoted in *The Choice Is Always Ours*, p. 393.

13. Don and Carla Aycock, *Not Quite Heaven* (Lima, Ohio: C.S.S. Publishing Co., 1981), pp. 8, 14.

14. Don M. Aycock, *The E. Y. Mullins Lectures On Preaching* (Washington, D.C.: University Press of America, 1980). And, Don M. Aycock, ed. *Preaching With Purpose and Power: Selected Mullins Lectures* (Macon, Ga.: Mercer University Press, 1982).

15. *Apathy In The Pew: Ministering To The Uninvolved* (Johnson City, Tn.: Institute of Social Sciences and Arts, Inc., 1983).

16. *Symbols of Salvation* (Nashville, Tennessee: Braodman Press, 1982).

17. Harry Emerson Fosdick, *The Living of These Days* (New York: Harper and Row, 1956), p. 89.

18. Ibid., p. 90.

19. Ibid., p. 121.

20. Harry Edward Neal tells the genesis of this story in his *Nonfiction: From Idea To Published Book* (New York: Wilfred Funk, Inc., 1964), p. 25.

21. The book which explained this system to the authors is *The Minister's Filing System*, by Paul Gericke. (Grand Rapids: Baker Book House, 1971.)

Chapter 3

MECHANICS: GETTING IT ON PAPER

MECHANICS: GETTING IT ON PAPER

An editor at a well-known publishing house once advised his authors, "Work hard, type neatly, consult the dictionary, pay heed to grammar, and don't write in the hope of making money or becoming famous, but because you are *compelled* to write."[1] Being compelled to write by some inner drive is laudable, but even a writer so compelled still faces the mundane question, "How do I get it all on paper?" No one can offer an exact formula for "getting it all on paper." But we can suggest some guidelines to follow and traps to avoid so you do not have to preface your works as Edward Gibbon (1737-1794) once did: "Unprovided with original learning, unformed in the habits of thinking, unskilled in the arts of composition, I resolved to write a book."[2]

Mechanics

Writing is not nearly so mysterious as mechanical. Logic and form lie behind the presentation of ideas via words. Your task, as an author, is to find that logic and form and to utilize them as vehicles for your thoughts. How is this done? Of course you have to have a central idea first. Most nonfiction books center around a theme or a topic. Many inexperienced writers forget this fact and put down on paper virtually any ideas that come to them, seemingly in a random fashion . They then call the end result a book. But it is much too loose and unorganized to be considered a unified piece of writing.

Sherman R. Hanson, longtime editor of The Bethany Press, has noted, "The major problem with most beginning religion writers is their assumption that if their work has a pious sound, it is publishable. To do worthful writing in this field people must STUDY and THINK CRITICALLY; their writing must show evidence of responsible work in ecclesiological and theological disciplines."[3]

The beginning writer's tendency simply to write whatever comes naturally without putting it in a logical order results sometimes in an author getting a muddled idea of what his topic and who his intended audience is. James E. Ruark, Senior Editor at Zondervan Publishing House, says, "Some religious books will appeal to a wide range of Christian readers because of the subject matter; others really have a targeted audience. It is important for the writer to keep the audience in mind. For example, sometimes a book dealing with counseling problems will try to address both the counselor and the counselee; but this does not make sense. The writer might decide whether the book is one which the counselor should use or the person who needs the counseling. In the case of the latter, a book addressed to the counselee might prove to be one that a counselor will give to the client, and therefore it still has a market in both audiences—but is addressed to one."[4]

The counsel of one other editor will be helpful here. Leslie H. Stobbe, Editorial Director of Here's Life Publishers, realizes that many writers tackling their first book-length project tend to put ideas on paper somewhat randomly as the ideas occur to them. "When done, they send a manuscript off to a publisher. They often do not have a clear idea of who their market is, so they do not target the book for a specific market. They do not have a clear outline, revealing what they want to have happen in the mind/life of the reader. They are more concerned with the information they feel they 'must share,' rather than with meeting a 'felt need' in the market."[5]

Having a clear idea of exactly what you are trying to say, and to whom you wish to say it is essential in writing a non-fiction religious book. But once that central idea is firmly and coherently in mind, the ways of expanding and exploring it are legion.

Brainstorm

One helpful way to begin is to ask yourself questions like, "What do I already know about this subject? Why does this topic intrigue me? What have my experiences been?" Brainstorm it. Use your memory. As you do so, write down every idea that occurs to you. At this point pay no attention to how the thoughts flow or how your notes look. You can rearrange and tidy these up later. For the present, simply let your mind produce everything it has on your subject. That subject might be, for example, how God works with people in times of crisis. As you think about it for awhile, you may recall a time when your Aunt Jane nearly died, and how her church prayed and God brought her safely through the crisis. You might remember personal situations where you felt God was truly present and working.

Then use your imagination. What can you imagine about your subject? How can you envision things being different? We are not suggesting you "invent" experiences, but merely see things from different perspectives, which is what using the imagination is all about.

Outline and Research

Probably you will not get too far before you exhaust your own reservoir of knowledge on any subject. Your next move will be to begin to research the topic at hand. Go to a local library and look through the card catalog for other books on your general topic. You will want to do this before you get too far along with your project. Someone else may have recently written a book on the exact topic you have in mind. If so, you will want to give some serious thought about working on another topic, or at least shifting the focus of your work. Remember that you want your book to fill an actual need in the market which no other book fills.

Read everything you can get your hands on related to your

subject. Make careful notes as you go along. If you quote some-one, double-check that you have done so correctly. Be sure to get the full bibliographic information from the book because you will need it later to identify the source. The purpose of this research is not to rehash what someone else has already said, but to lay the backdrop for what *you* are going to say. Someone once snidely commented that the art of writing history books is the art of taking bits and pieces out of books that no one has read and putting them into a book that no one will read. This is not what you want to do.

Reading as background study will give you an overall perspective and "bird's eye" view of the field. It will furnish you a body of knowledge about your subject on which to draw and, if necessary, refute and revise.

Finding suitable material in a general library, especially in the field of religion, might be a problem. Try to locate the library of a local college with a religion department, or a seminary or Bible school. If you do not have access to any such school, you might consider using the services of a lending library. An excellent one is the General Theological Library, located at 14 Beacon Street, Boston, Massachusetts, 02108. This is a non-sectarian library which is well-stocked and gladly lends books, journals and periodicals to anyone who asks for them. The best thing about it is that the services are free (although they do accept donations). If you write this library, they will put you on a mailing list to receive regular notices listing new accessions. Their *Bulletin* is published quarterly with a subscription fee of $10.00 per year. Another library service is the Kesler Circulating Library, Vanderbilt Divinity School, Nashville, Tennessee, 37203.

After reading books and articles on your subject, begin working on a *plan* of writing, an outline. Any good handbook on grammar will give you detailed instructions on outlining. You may not care to go into great detail, but you will need to break up your topic into small, manageable portions. That is the purpose of the outline. After all, you can eat an elephant if you take it one bite at a time.

Let's consider the outline for this book. First, we have both read many books on the subject of writing. Most of these were read, by the way, for pure edification. We simply enjoyed reading them, but as we read we realized that not a single book, so far as we could tell, was devoted to the matter of writing nonfiction religious books. That is why this book has been written.

Work on the outline began by jotting down areas and ideas which a book such as this should cover. This outline was reworked and changed several times until it reached the present form. Initially, it was felt that the first chapter should discuss briefly the process of writing and attempt to justify the book. At first we thought this chapter should be very involved, talking about the technicalities of writing. This idea was changed, however, to focus on a "how to" approach.

We felt that chapter 2 should center in on ideas from which to write. How does a writer get his or her ideas? Where do they come from? How are they preserved? And so on.

Getting your ideas on paper is usually a difficult process, so we thought the third chapter on mechanics would be necessary and helpful.

Most new writers admit they are scared or intimidated by editors, so chapters four and five attempt to "demythologize" these ivory tower types. We contacted more than two dozen editors and publishing executives known to one or both of us either personally or through correspondence and asked them to give us their views and counsel for beginning writers. They were very helpful, giving much more information than we could possibly use.

Beginning writers might be confused by book contracts. We felt contract samples explained in detail in chapter 6 would alleviate most of the confusion.

Novice writers need to know the basic research tools, so chapter 7 is devoted to explaining what these tools are.

Chapter 8 is dedicated to what every beginning author really wants to know—book markets. We include some of the better religious book markets here, along with the names of the editors to contact.

We felt the final materials in the book should be devoted to offering the beginning writer further help. For this reason, we included an annotated bibliography. While this book focuses on the writing of nonfiction *books*, we nevertheless wished to add some other material about non-books. We wanted to touch on those many kinds of writing genre which exist: straightforward articles, short devotional pieces, paraphrases, parables, sermons, book reviews, as well as curriculum. Lastly, since new and established writers alike constantly ask publishers for style manuals, we wanted to include a sample manual in the book. (The one we included is our own publisher's style guide for writers and editors, so the reader will have a fairly standard manual for reference.)

You can see from all this that the process of developing an outline is not secret or mysterious. It is logical and developmental. Besides that, it is plain hard work.

Flesh out the outline

Once you have done sufficient research on your subject and have established a working outline, the time has come for applying the seat of the pants to the seat of the chair. It is time to begin writing.

This is not only the point which is the most difficult to describe but also the most tricky on which to advise. Writing has to do with the individual expression of *your* unique ideas. It is personal, and as such, no one can tell you exactly how to write. However, some general advice on style might be helpful.

Margaret K. McElderry, former editor of Harcourt, Brace and World, instructs, "Don't try to tailor your writing to any specific 'market.' First, have something you really *want* to write about, whether it's fiction or nonfiction. Then write to the best of your ability, to please yourself."[6] All editors would say think for yourself, and write what you think honestly.

The temptation to try to make your book *sound* like a

"religious" book is especially strong. To think that by using the language of Zion your book will be helpful or saleable is a mistake. King James language was perfect for people who lived in the sixteenth century, but it is not sharp or effective today. All the sharp edges are worn smooth from years of use. Sherman R. Hanson, editor of The Bethany Press, notes that "writers must master the craft of writing. Sweetness and piosity just will not make up for sloppy literary styling."[7] Leslie H. Stobbe, with Here's Life Publishers, also mentioned that writers must learn to express themselves with uniqueness and clarity, since, he noted, "many beginners do not have their writing skills to produce a unique, eminently readable product."[8]

James Hoover, Associate Editor at InterVarsity Press, wrote that some beginning writers seem to prefer flair without substance or substance without flair. The key is to find the right combination.[9]

The issue here is individual writing style. But for a writing style to be truly "personal," one must continually work at it. Wishing and dreaming about being a writer won't help. Many editors will tell you that most writers simply have not written enough of *anything* to find their own styles. One editor says he gets at least one manuscript each week on the end times by some "scholar" who thinks he or she has it all figured out. (These are never actual academicians, but people who have chosen the end times as their pet area.) But the editor realizes that these aspiring authors understand neither eschatology (the theological doctrine of final things) nor do they understand much about writing, for the writing styles on most of these manuscripts are all but rescuable.

If you want to write, then you must write. Write a journal for yourself. Write short articles for magazines. Work on some book reviews for a local paper. Write pieces for your church newsletter or bulletin. Learn how to use words and to express yourself in sharp, unique ways. The thing is to systematically get your thoughts *down on paper*. When you can take a sharply focused idea and expand the idea into 30,000 words, then you are ready to write a book. In fact, it *is* a book. The only tools you need are the common ones: words, paper, a typewriter. But you must want to keep at it, for writing is hard work.

Just as you outline the book as a whole, also outline each chapter. This will facilitate your flow of thoughts as you move through the actual work of putting the words on paper. If your chapter will be twelve pages, for example, you might have six subdivisions or points on your outline for that chapter. If each is worthy of equal treatment, then you may attempt to write two pages on each. Most will find it much easier to write this way, knowing that they do not have to simply fill up twelve blank pages, but that two or three pages can be completed before moving on to expand another aspect of the main idea.

Revising

Once you have finished the book, do not immediately celebrate or ship it off to a publisher. Invariably, it is not ready. You still need to revise it. This, like the writing itself, is difficult work and is done according to individual preference. Some writers work on a few pages and then revise them. Others finish the entire manuscript and then revise the complete work.

In either case, it is revision which separates the amateurs from the pros. Donald Murray describes this difference:

> When the beginning writer completes his first draft, he usually reads it through to correct typographical errors and considers the job of writing done. When the professional writer completes his first draft, he usually feels he is at the start of the writing process. Now that he has a draft, he can begin writing.[10]

Elton Trueblood wrote of his method of revising his writing:

> I can support Dr. (Samuel) Johnson's famous words, "The production of something where nothing was before, is an act of greater energy than the expansion or decoration of the thing produced." The perennial advice, therefore, is "Invent first and embellish later." I find that my scissors are among the most used of the literary tools on my desk because, after a chapter is in typescript, it becomes obvious to me that certain lines will

fit better in some place other than that in which they were originally located. Accordingly, on the second typing, one page may be made up of a number of small parts clipped together.[11]

Leave the material you want to revise for awhile. Let it get "cold" in your thinking. This way it will seem fresh when you read it later. Knowing it less intimately after leaving it for a time, you will be able to view it more objectively.

Read you work aloud for mistakes of all sorts—grammar errors, misspelled words, misplaced modifiers, continuity and pace. Cut out non-essential words. Smooth out and tighten sentences and make transitions logical and natural.[12]

Once you have the material in what you consider "final" form, you might have a friend read it to see if he or she can spot errors of thought or style which escaped your attention. Choose this reader with care, however. You would not want a less than careful reader to proof your material.

Typing

Type out your final product (or have someone else do it) with great care. Edd Rowell, Jr., Editor-in-Chief of Mercer University Press, says that many beginning writers err at this point and seriously hurt their chances of having a publisher accept their manuscript. When the material is forwarded to the publisher, he says, "the manuscripts should be typed, double-spaced on the page (this includes footnotes, bibliography, and all other manuscript contents), with adequate margins on the page. Of course, double-spacing requires twice the amount of paper, but it increases efficiency tenfold."[13]

Some writers will try to grab the editor's attention by using peculiar materials—like buff paper and green type. But look at your manuscript from the editor's viewpoint—would *you* really give serious attention to such a manuscript? Use good quality, white 8½ x 11 paper, and type with a pica or elite typewriter always with a black ribbon. If you hurt the editor's eyes, or otherwise make it difficult to peruse your typescript, you don't have much of a chance to sell your book. (Be sure to look at the "Preparation of the Manuscript" section in the sample style guide included in this book.)

Recap

Remember that the mechanics of getting your ideas onto paper can be the most frustrating part of the writing process, but if you keep a few simple guidelines in mind, you can get through this difficult period.

Focus the major theme of your book sharply. Answer these questions in your own mind: Exactly what am I trying to say in this book? Why am I trying to say it? Who will read it? Why will they read my book instead of someone else's?

Refine and shape your ideas carefully. Do not yield to the temptation simply to dump them onto the paper as they occur to you.

Brainstorm your topic. Call to mind what you already know about your subject.

Draw up a tentative outline based on research. After you have finished researching, revise the outline if necessary and write your first draft. Try to develop your own style of writing.

Revise the manuscript. Read it over several times to make sure your ideas are logical and clear and your sentences are smooth. Correct spelling and grammar errors. Read the manuscript aloud to check for continuity and pace. Revise again and again, if necessary.

Type the final product with a good typewriter. Use good 8½ x 11 paper.

When you have done all of this, you are certainly ready to begin contacting publishers about your work, if you have not done so by now. In any case, the next two chapters will help you contact and negotiate with book editors of publishing firms.

NOTES

1. Dan Wickenden, quoted by David Raffclock, *Writing For The Markets* (New York: Funk and Wagnalls, 1969), p.79.

2. Edward Gibbon, in *Peter's Quotation*, Laurence J. Peter (New York: Bantam Books, 1979) p.544.

3. Personal Correspondence.

4. Personal Correspondence.

5. Personal Correspondence.

6. Margaret K. McElderry, in *Writing For The Markets*, p.84.

7. Personal Correspondence.

8. Personal Correspondence.

9. Personal Correspondence.

10. Donald M. Murray, "The Maker's Eye: Revising Your Own Manuscripts," *The Writer*, October 1973, p.14.

11. Elton Trueblood, *While It Is Day* (New York: Harper and Row, 1974), p. 64.

12. Helpful material on rewriting is David S. McCarthy, *Practical Guide For The Christian Writer* (Valley Forge, PA.: Judson Press, 1983), pp.88-90.

13. Personal Correspondence.

Chapter 4

EDITORS: HOW TO CONTACT AND WHAT TO SEND

EDITORS: HOW TO CONTACT AND WHAT TO SEND

When you have finished your book, or at least an expanded outline with a couple of sample chapters, you face a crucial juncture: whom to contact in order to get the book published. Which publisher should see your material? How does a beginning writer contact an editor? What should he or she say? What should accompany the initial contact? This chapter will answer these and similar questions.

Some writers feel they must finish a manuscript in its entirety before they then ship it willy-nilly to any publisher they can find. This only rarely works, and there is a much more logical and methodical way to approach it. You, as a writer, obviously need to learn the art of writing. But you also need to learn the art of selling your writing. Study the kinds of books various publishers issue. Browse religious bookstores to check out recent publications. Read the catalogs and bulletins of the publishers. Some will send them to you free of charge, and some even have authors' guidelines. Check with them to see what is available.

By all means, consult the books published by the various houses. Get acquainted with a publisher's tone or style of publishing. When you do, you will know that a firm like Zondervan Publishers or Baker Book House would be more likely to issue a thoroughgoing evangelical book than would Westminster or Beacon Press. Harvest House or Fleming

Revell, for examples, would be less likely to publish serious, scholarly titles than would, say, Wm. B. Eerdmans Company, Fortress Press, or Oxford University Press. Knowing the publisher after studying their book line, you would probably not want to send an issues-oriented book written from a liberal perspective to Crossway Books—but you might want to try Harper and Row.

Query

Once you have decided upon a publisher, send a query letter to the appropriate editor. Most publishers appreciate the query approach, and do not wish to receive unsolicited manuscripts in the mail. You can find the editor's name and address of the publisher in publications such as *The Writer's Handbook*, *The Writer's Market*, or *The Literary Marketplace*. Chapters 7 and 8 will have more information on these publications and markets.

In that letter, introduce yourself to the editor. Tell him or her who you are and what your qualifications are for writing on your topic. Give the editor a brief description of the contents of your book, mention how it differs from other books on the subject, and gauge the readership for which the manuscript was written. Be sure to mention your interpretation of the importance of the book. Send a sample chapter or two, along with the outline. An editor does not usually need to read an entire manuscript in order to know if the book fits in with their list, or whether the material is actually publishable.

Always enclose with any material a self-addressed, stamped envelope. This will facilitate the response of the editor and/or the return of your material. After you do this, wait! An editor may need up to three months to reply to your query, although most do so within a few weeks.

From the "horses" mouth

The best way to find out what editors need to see from an aspiring author is simply to ask them. The responses below are helpful comments from various editors which are taken from personal correspondence to the authors.

Roland Seboldt, Director of Book Development at Augsburg Publishing House, has these comments for writers: "All letters should be clearly written and typed to gain the attention of the editor with a minimum amount of time expended. Publishing houses such as ours receive 5000 manuscripts and queries per year. This means that the ones clearly expressing their purpose and market target will get the most immediate attention."

Edd Rowell, Jr., Editor-in-Chief of Mercer University Press, notes,"the most important thing in insuring that an editor will read a manuscript is that the author has chosen a timely subject and then has dealt with it carefully in the way the subject has been researched and written. Secondly, a clean and well-prepared manuscript . . . is the best insurance that it will be read."

The editor of The Bethany Press, Sherman R. Hanson, offers a warning to writers at the point of queries:"They [beginning writers] can't expect their work to be seriously read by an editor if their thinking is fuzzy and their writing inane."

Jack Gargiulo, Director of Religious Education Services of Argus Communications, advises writers to give only a brief summary of their work along with an outline. He also urges authors to point out how the book project developed (was it experiential, in the classroom, research?).

Daniel Van't Kerkhoff, Chief Editor at Baker Book House, cautions that while submission of ideas can be by query letters alone, authors really should include a couple of chapters so the editor can see their writing style, idea development, and so on.

Senior Editor James E. Ruark at Zondervan Publishers offers very substantial advice: "Being honest, specific, and courteous goes a long way. Honest: Perhaps the writer feels 'the Lord inspired me to write this book and send it to you,' but subjective guidance has limitations; every manuscript must stand on its merits when it is evaluated. Specific: Tell the editor why this book is different and why it merits consideration. If a writer is doing a book about marriage, what makes it different in content or approach from half a zillion other books already in the bookstore? There are different approaches or specific problems that are publishable; make sure you have one. Courteous: Don't impugn the publisher's integrity; be neat and tactful in your presentation. Also, should you get a rejection letter that is obviously a standard form, try to understand that although the publisher might like to offer specific criticisms, it is not usually possible to do so. Any specific criticism should be taken as an encouraging sign that the proposal had enough merit to warrant a little extra attention; but publishers who accept unsolicited manuscripts simply cannot respond to each one with an individualized letter.''

Leslie H. Stobbe, former Editorial Director of Christian Herald Books and now with Here's Life Publishers, advises authors to include in their proposals a two-page selling synopsis which describes the target market along with the ''felt need'' they are meeting.

Associate Editor at InterVarsity Press, James Hoover, notes that ''a cleanly-typed, well-written letter is much more persuasive than one that is sloppy and poorly-written. An editor cannot help making some judgment of an author's writing ability based on his or her letter of inquiry. A letter of inquiry should give some indication of the author's qualifications as well as the reasons for writing about the proposed topic. I find a low-key approach that nevertheless convinces me of the value of the author's ideas much more persuasive than a snow job concerning the author's anticipated sales for the book.''

The late Robert W. Hill, who was Editor-in-Chief of Association Press (part of New Century Publishers), told authors to be careful to define their work in a short, to-the-point letter. Tell, as clearly as possible, exactly what your book is.

Echoing a similar sentiment is Donald E. Pugh, Senior Editor of Regal Books. He likes to see query letters which answer these questions: Why another book? Why this particular book? What makes this book deserve a place in the market? What qualifies the author to write about this subject? What would make someone pick it up?

Joe S. Johnson, Editor of the Inspirational Books line at Broadman Press, offers this advice: "There is nothing in particular the writer can do to insure that an editor will read his/her idea or manuscript, carefully or uncarefully. The best means of egging the editor into reading the manuscript is to make it so rare and so unique that the editor, for his sanity, will have to read it." Further, "The best means of assuring that an editor will read and read carefully your material is that your material be prepared convincingly and attractively—well-typed, no misspellings, no punctuation errors, no sloppiness. And by all means attach a synopsis and/or outline of your material."

The Managing Editor at Crossroad Publishing Company (formerly the religious publishing arm of Seabury Press), Frank Oveis, reminds authors to "study the various religious publishers. Follow their ads and reviews in the religious media as well as in professional journals such as *The Christian Bookseller*, *Bookstore Journal*, and *Religious Book Review*. Then determine which publishers are likely to be interested in your manuscript. In my experience, many writers haven't the foggiest idea *what* sort of religious books we at Crossroad . . . do."

Martha Perry, Production Editor at Liguori Publications, notes an interesting predicament many beginning writers fall into: "Some of the major problems beginning writers seem to have in writing nonfiction religious books are opposite extremes. Many writers present their subject in such an erudite manner that the normal 'lay' person is completely at a loss in understanding the points presented. At the other side of the pole, other authors belabor a point until the reader is made to feel rather dense. The primary view of the author should be to communicate—be concise, not clever. Most editors are not looking for another Andrew Greeley nor another Erma Bombeck."

Ms. Perry, along with many of the other editors represented, notes, "To insure that your material will be read, it MUST BE NEAT. If an editor has to read through coffee stains, smudges, and crossed out words, he will soon give up." Writers are urged to use pica font because script or elite type is hard reading for eyes that may be tired from wading through similar material.

She continues, "Another point to remember when presenting your material or query letter is to use a professional approach. State your intention, give some personal background concerning yourself and your proposed project, and rest your case. Avoid wordiness, as most editors are too busy to read page after page of chattiness."

Keith M. Bailey, formerly Managing Editor at Christian Publications, points out that beginning writers often forget to seek creativity. "They are rehashing old themes on which considerable work has been done in the past, or they are writing in areas where they are not well qualified. Therefore, the material lacks substance and credibility." When contacting an editor, the writer should take care with his or her query letter: "It should not be a mimeographed sheet, such as I often find coming to my desk. It should have attached to it at least a two-page resume of the book, table of contents, and sample chapter, so that the editor has some idea of the nature of the book."

Robert H. Hawkins, President of Harvest House Publishers, states that many beginning writers do not know how to write in a simple style that will interest "the average person on the street." A book will have trouble selling if it is not in "lay language" or interesting enough for the mass of people.

The recent textbook editor at Moody Press, Philip Rawley, writes,"First, many beginning writers fail to research the market carefully and as a result offer a publisher a book on a subject that has already been saturated with books. Along with this, new writers often fail to research their *subject* well, resulting in a work that is shallow and doesn't deal adequately with the data available on the particular topic."

Mr. Rawley continues, "A new author can help himself with a publisher by asking what that publisher needs, and tailoring his query to those needs." He further agrees that most editors like to receive a query letter as opposed to a full manuscript.

Editor John Sloan of Multnomah Press points out some of the weaknesses beginning authors must work to overcome. These include "a lack of in-depth vocabulary resources—and sometimes a lack of adequate research to back up the material that is being written. If the research is adequate, many times the writer will face another problem: the writing of material that sounds too stilted or academic."

He continues, "The ability to submit a well-written query with paragraph summaries of each chapter and an overall synopsis of the book is a must. This will get your idea quickly before the editor's eyes and into his thought patterns as to whether this book will fit into the publishing schedule and philosophy of that particular house."

Beacon Hill Press's Editor Betty Fuhrman responds that "basically there are too many inexperienced authors who are writing in areas beyond their ability. Many send in poorly written queries which turn off potential publishers at the start. There are also too many with below average ideas who try to write because they want to help somebody profit from their experience. This is a good motive but unfortunately does not insure a quality manuscript."

Bruce Nygren is the Managing Editor of Trade Books at Thomas Nelson Publishers. He points out that inadequate research determining existing books on a particular subject is often a problem for a novice author. Another problem is generally poor writing skills. Mr. Nygren feels sure, however, that editors will pay attention to book ideas which are fresh and creative.

Consensus

By now you have realized that various items have been mentioned repeatedly. These include the following:

Neatness—make all correspondence, manuscripts, and

outlines as neat and attractive as possible. Remember, if you are competing with roughly 5000 queries in a year, you need to have an edge. Neatness is that edge.

Clarity—have in your mind exactly what you want to write about, with a clear idea of who will read your book. Express yourself as clearly as possible.

Timely subject—be aware of what people are interested in reading; do not rehash subjects which have been done *ad nauseum.*

Outline and/or summary—editors would rather read a two or three page abstract and detailed outline than a 200 page manuscript.

Honesty—do not try to "snow" editors about your work; a little humility about its value goes a long way.

Courtesy—editors, despite popular opinion, are people, too; treat them as such.

Creativity—write in such a way as to make sure the editor, and ultimately, the reading public, will *have* to read the book.

Awareness—know who publishes what type of material. Do not waste your time sending a query letter and additional material to a publisher who will not view your project as consistent with his or her acquisition goals.

Discouragement

As you begin fleshing out your ideas and searching for a suitable publisher for your material, you will no doubt often be told, "Sorry, but we're unable to express interest." Rejection slips or letters can injure a writer's pride almost quicker than anything else. Writers must develop thick skins! Some editors reject an idea or manuscript with form letters, most often because they simply can't respond to each individual inquiry. Others will write nice letters and perhaps explain exactly why the idea was turned down. Some will even offer advice as to revision or other possible publishers you should contact.

No writer who has ever written much has ever survived without receiving rejection letters. You will not escape either.

But remember this—*do not get discouraged!* If your idea is worthy and your execution of it is good, someone will eventually express a publishing interest in your book. We speak as experts on rejection slips. Author Aycock has received almost as many rejection slips as Editor Goss has sent! On the first book Aycock published, his manuscript was turned down 18 times. His second book was accepted by the first publisher. But his third one was turned down by 87 publishers! One would normally wonder if a project rejected at 87 houses would be worth pursuing, but this manuscript was a unique anthology of lectures on preaching by some of this century's greatest preachers. Many publishers simply would not handle anthologies. But he knew the manuscript was worthy, so he kept trying. He received a contract from publisher number 88. This book went on to become the featured selection of a large religious book club.

Don't give up!

Chapter 5

SUBSTANCE: WHAT DO EDITORS WANT?

SUBSTANCE: WHAT DO EDITORS WANT?

In the preceding chapter, we offered some of the comments and ideas which religious book editors related to submitting synopses and manuscripts. We will now expand on this and pass along other general comments and opinions editors have on writing. As before, the editors will speak for themselves. We think that you will find their advice both illuminating and practical.

Augsburg's Roland Seboldt had this to say on writing non-fiction religious books: "Books which speak to the needs and aspirations of people will always have value. Books that help people solve problems, grow in faith and see a new perspective in life need to be written in every generation to apply the old truths of Scripture and the Christian tradition to the world in which we live." In addition to giving advice on what kinds of books need to be written, Mr. Seboldt also notes, "My first suggestion [to beginning writers] is always to get started by writing articles, short pieces, letters to the editor, newspaper columns, items for the parish paper of the congregation. Generally, writers do not start by writing books first. First writers do short pieces in other media and then gradually develop their skills for book publishing."

We asked these editors what kinds of religious books they thought would be selling in the near future. Edd Rowell, Jr., of the Mercer University Press, mentions that, "the areas of interest in nonfiction religious books is so broad that it is difficult to say in a few words what are the most interesting subjects today. In general, however, I would say that those books of most interest are the ones which deal with timely subjects in a readable and authoritative way. Personally, I would like to see some good scholarly treatments of evangelism, religious conversion, and the whole spectrum of the new right movement. Of course, well-researched treatments of biblical studies and church history are of perennial interest."

Editor at Harper & Row, Roy M. Carlisle, has this to say: "What am I looking for today as a book editor? People. People who are experiencing the heights and depths of life. People who are willing to be in touch with their own passions and concerns. People who connect with the deeper currents of life in general and, more particularly, life in the Spirit. All of us are drawn to these types of people. And when they combine this passion for life, this sensitivity to God's call to "come further up and further in," with the habits of constant reading, reflection, and writing they are on the way to becoming an insightful and thoughtful writer. They have also discovered that creativity grows out of the soils of these disciplines. I find myself depending upon these people to tell me what should be written; and they rely on me to encourage them in their writing, to work with them to develop and express their ideas in publishable form. My prayer is that many will be called and many chosen."

Sherman R. Hansen, of The Bethany Press, reminds beginning writers that, "Books that help readers think responsibly about the church's life and mission, and others that show 'how to' get at things like evangelism and stewardship will always attract readers." Further, "Aspiring authors, like aspiring architects, engineers and astronomers, just have to work. They have to study, learn, grow and become able to check their 'notions' against 'realities' and 'truths'. If they are to fulfill their PROMISE they must labor patiently and persistently, over an extended period of time."

Jack Gargiulo, with Argus Communications, feels that

authors who write in areas of prayer, spirituality, and scripture will probably be on target as far as having an audience. He also reminds aspiring authors never to give up. Seek various publishers. Try to get part of your book published in magazines if nothing else works out.

Baker's Dan Van't Kerkhoff notes, "It is difficult to define what type of nonfiction books sell well. There are many categories. Basically, the author as well as the publisher should take a hard look at the marketing potential. This means that he must connect with a broad general need among his designated readership. Autobiographies are hardly worthwhile. The author should be familiar with the religious bookstore through talking with bookstore managers. He should also scan the latest catalogs by the largest religious publishers. Scanning book advertising in such magazines as *Moody Monthly* will also indicate the subject areas that are being published successfully."

From Doubleday's Religion Department, Executive Editor Robert T. Heller offers these cautions: "The standard remains the same regardless of subject—you have to have something to say; content is more important than style. Too many nonfiction books are published today that are simply expanded magazine articles which are ephemeral in nature, outdated at publication. The value that a book offers to a buyer is a full treatment of a subject from an author who, at the least, is qualified to write on said subject and who, better yet, has achieved a certain notoriety in his or her chosen field. Clever titles help, good clear organization and felicitous use of language make the reading experience more enjoyable, but without a subject worthy of serious treatment, it is all a pencil with a broken point. It's apparent to me that, particularly in that segment of the religious market labeled Evangelical, we are in a period of asking deeper questions about faith and life. There is always a place for inspiration, but, for the moment, information questions take precedence. The important task for the nonfiction religious book is to take unchanging truth and integrate it with our changing lives—a worthy challenge."

The concerns of the scholarly publishing community are varied, of course, but can be represented by the comments of Jon Pott, Vice-President and Editor-in-Chief of Wm. B. Eerdmans Publishing Company: "War and peace will continue as a major issue, especially now that one needn't be a bearded or braless placard-carrying peacenik to be worried about it. The literature will probably be somewhat less rhetorical now and more reflective, sophisticated, and nuanced.

"Geopolitical concerns will also, I should think, remain big, perhaps eclipsing concerns for domestic hunger, poverty, and injustice. Racism doesn't seem a vital area to be writing in now unless one is able to do a compelling post-civil-rights analysis that really lays bare the deeper levels of racism that, many would argue, remain entrenched.

"As in the case of war and peace, much of the rhetoric on the women's issue and the church may also be spent. The next stage will be one of more subdued reflection and analysis, and also of proposing strategies for implementation.

"Another area I will be watching with considerable interest is that of medical ethics. Abortion will remain an issue, but lots of other questions relating to life and death will also be game for discussion.

"On the more strictly theological front, I should think that ecumenical matters will be important in many sectors—especially given a document like *Baptism, Eucharist and Ministry*. The more fundamentalist churches, of course, won't be much interested, but I think that interest will grow appreciably among a number of more ecumenically open evangelicals. In this connection, of course, any new books on the Lord's Supper may be relevant, as will books having to do with liturgy. I might say that I think the theological world is also probably ripe for a solid study in ecclesiology; not much has been done here that I can think of.

"I don't know where 'spirituality' is these days, except that it seems to be post-charismatic. My hunch is that the spiritual tradition associated with the Catholic and Episcopal traditions will be appropriated by more of the Protestant sector. Think of Henri Nouwen, to name perhaps the most visible symbol, and in a sense Richard Foster.

"Well, I've probably gone on far too long about what is far too obvious. Let me mention one more thing that is more general and possibly a bit less apparent. Given the conservative swing in this country, I wouldn't be surprised if even among liberals there won't be a growing appreciation for the virtues of responsibility and commitment. The modern family seems to be making something of a comeback; women's magazines seem not quite so glib about the joys of extra-marital affairs (more talk about lasting relationships); there seems in the air even among the chic a bit more sense that what feels good may in the long run be related to being disciplined and fulfilling obligations. A good sophisticated book about commitment would interest me."

Some editors find defining exactly what type of book sells well a bit difficult. James E. Ruark at Zondervan is one such editor. Speaking specifically about his own company, Mr. Ruark says," . . . our publishing program is broad enough that no single kind of book dominates our list; also, we are not a 'fad' publisher, although we of course are responsible to trends. Our backlist is very strong, and most of the books we publish are likely to have a pretty good life. . . . Another reason why this question (about what types of books sell well) is so difficult is that by the time I were to suggest a topic, we would probably have three manuscripts here for evaluation already. A look at our catalog would quickly reveal several main interests that we have, but there are many variations within these categories: Bible study, popular psychology, personal stories, and more professional and academic books including biblical language aids. I am more interested in knowing what an aspiring writer feels qualified to write about and what ideas he or she has."

Mr. Ruark also has advice on other topics of interest to beginning writers. "First, do your homework. Not only on your subject but in regards to the religious book marketplace in general. Establish your credibility. We receive many, many commentaries on the Book of Revelation or biblical prophecy that are subjective, redundant, and logically inadequate— and written by laypersons who have no qualifications, professionally speaking, to be writing on the subject.

"Second, plan to work hard. You don't find time to write a book, you make time. You can plan on more perspiration than inspiration, as Thomas Edison suggested. And as John Irving says, three ingredients necessary to be a writer are 'stamina, patience, and passion.'

"Third, don't look to writing as an easy way to make money. Established writers can gain a steady income from writing, but most religious book writers do it as an avocation even after they've achieved some success. The financial rewards are gratifying and important, but they are not the only reward; and often the amount of work necessary to achieve success involves a price. And often the money doesn't come quickly; in writing books, there is a waiting time before the book is off the press, and royalties may not be paid for up to a year after the book is published (your contract will give specifics on this).

"Fourth, keep trying. If rejection slips start piling up, reconsider what you are doing wrong or failing to do. Be open to constructive criticism from qualified critics. Your friends may like your work, but there's no risk in their telling you they like it; there is risk in their trying to critique it, and their evaluation may not really be qualified. If you have talent and take adequate steps to develop it, you will meet with success in time. Nothing makes a publisher happier than to receive a highly publishable work from an unknown writer. That is one of the best rewards and challenges of religious book publishing. We like to hear from you."

Leslie H. Stobbe at Here's Life has this thoughtful advice for new writers: "Every book that meets a broadly felt need will sell if written reasonably well. It's up to the author to be well enough read in daily newspapers, weekly or monthly magazines, and in frequent enough touch with people where they really live, to come up with 'trends'. A visit to a local Christian as well as secular bookseller is most helpful." Mr.

Stobbe also has this reminder: "Write to meet a genuine need, not to merely express yourself."

InterVarsity editor James Hoover echoes this advice: "Don't write to write. Write to say something. Write clearly, write personally and avoid jargon." Further, books of substance that capture the reading public's imagination will have a book-buying public. Also those which are "well-written, well-illustrated from a personal experience and well-thought-through from a biblical perspective."

Victor Books executive editor, James Adair, has this to share. "In regard to what beginning authors should consider writing in the area of nonfiction: If I were a beginning author, a person able to put words together like a good word carpenter, I think I'd leave my Ivory Tower and come down to earth. I'd look for a good story to tell and work with someone who has the story to make it into a good book. I'd not only assume the job of writing the manuscript but would become the agent in contacting publishers with a proposal and finally negotiating contracts for the project.

"The beginning author, in my opinion, has little chance of having his nonfiction published, as good as it may be, if he writes independently—unless he is an expert on the subject. Even experienced authors don't do well with books they write from research. I recall one well-known author who wrote a book on crucial issues relating to science that affect us. He interviewed a number of scientists but the book didn't do well at all. Now, if he had written the book for someone with a name, someone people respected for his/her expertise, the book likely would have done much better. I don't mean to say beginning writers should give up on doing nonfiction of their own. But I would encourage them to think of creating books for those with expertise on subjects, people who are too busy to write or not gifted as word carpenters. Often a royalty split of some sort can be worked out, with an advance to help put bread on the table while the project is under way.

"But the beginning writer should probably not tackle a book until he/she has successfully written many newspaper and magazine articles. Serve an apprenticeship first. As for topics for books for the future, science, family, money, survival. Plus many subjects relating to living the Christian life, that help Christians solve problems that confront them.''

The late Chief Editor of Association Press, Robert W. Hill, believed that books with some degree of inspiration would always sell fairly well. He also said, ''My advice to any author is to think out clearly and present on paper the skeleton of the work. Then flesh out this bare outline with detailed major considerations. Write clearly and to the point. The chips will then fall where they may.''

Writers are always interested in *how* an editor goes about making publishing decisions. Asked to comment on what kinds of religious books will be selling in the near future, Wendell Hawley, Vice-President and Editor-in-chief at Tyndale House Publishers, shared his thoughts. ''Like anyone else in the predicting business, one would like to have a foolproof crystal ball which would give infallible information. Since such an invaluable tool is not in my possession, I will launch out with a few guesstimations. On many different occasions I have found it very worthwhile in trying to assess a current situation or a future possibility, to take a long look back. This, I find, often clears our perspective, as we try to visualize the possibilities of the future. Looking back over past best-seller lists, I find that various books fall into different categories. I try to analyze the books of yesteryear by saying, 'What proved to be a fad, and what proved to have sustained readership appeal?' Viewing the best-seller list over a number of years, I try to see if there is a pattern of sales with various topics. I ask myself, 'What seems to sell 'on its own' and what requires much author visibility to sell the book?' Looking for answers to these questions often gives me insight as to the kind of manuscript or book I will be looking for at some point in the future. For instance, in the last fifty years we have had several cycles of interest in prophetic books. I believe that we are on the verge of yet another upswing in readership interest on prophecy.

"As I look at the present list of books, I asked myself a number of questions, such as, 'What is the outstanding book in any given subject area, and what makes that book unique, and, if the book has weaknesses, can we find a writer who can improve on the subject matter?' I try to watch for areas which seem to already have too many books on that given topic. Sometimes I receive a manuscript from a writer saying that they researched the area and couldn't find anything on this given topic, so they decided to write a book on the subject. Many times I could give the writer the names of a dozen books selling quite well in the bookstore on that very subject. Which leads me to the next question I am always asking myself. 'What areas seem to always absorb another book?' And I find at least two areas which seem to always allow for yet another book on the subject. That is books on motivation, and books on the family. Both subject areas, of course, will need to be written on by authorities in the field.

"In the religious area, I think two things are evolving. One, there is a spirit of contemplation and deeper devotional living than what seemed to be apparent in recent years. I believe there will be an interest in books on holy living, walking with God, fellowship with God, the 'deeper life' appeal. There also seems to me to be a realistic spirit of ecumenicity as it relates to various religious groups within the Christian framework. Books which relate to Christians getting along together as believers, I believe, will sell better than polemic books arguing the superiority of one doctrinal persuasion as better than another.

"In summary, then, I look to see an increase in prophetic books, a continued strong interest in books on the family, motivational books, devotional books, and good wholesome books which may be termed diversionary reading."

Regal's Donald E. Pugh advises the beginning writer, "Take it one step at a time. Get in print in magazines first. Often a publisher will contact the writer of an article to have it expanded into a book. Do your homework. Put your best foot forward. 'You never have a second chance to make a first impression'."

Frank Oveis of Crossroad Publishing muses that, especially for newer writers, "Fads and modes are easy enough to spot. The problem isn't types and genres, it's quality."

Broadman Press's Joe Johnson says that areas of concern in publishing change from year to year. For example, "At present we are emphasizing sound doctrine and church growth/evangelism. When we steer clear of our middle-of-the-road market, we make a mistake. Right now our best-sellers are sermons by viable preachers, books with unusual stories and testimonies, and self-help books. That could change, of course. We ran through a period of extreme interest in the Spirit-filled life, but that emphasis is on the wane. Five years ago renewal was all the rage. We seldom publish renewal-type books now."

Mr. Johnson offers some very helpful general advice for beginners on the substance of books and other matters. "(1) Keep on writing, whether or not you are published. Real writers write and write and write, even if it is only for their personal edification. (2) Refine what you submit. Shame on you if you write an editor: 'This is just a rough draft. This is not my best.' I don't want to waste my time on rough drafts. I want good stuff, not junk. (3) Spell out the facts about your manuscript—purpose for writing, intended market, possible uses of the book, selling points, promotion and advertising ideas. (4) Introduce yourself, if you're a new writer. Send a well-written biographical sketch. List your writing credits, if any. I appreciate honesty. 'I have written only one article for publication,' one lady wrote. I appreciated her candor. (5) Be kind and polite. Editors are human, too. Yes, they're at the mercy of authors in this business, believe it or not. Going around an editor to his superiors is not going to help matters. Intimidation is not going to work. After all, if an editor recommends your book, and it launches you in a successful career—and opens up new vistas for you—the editor is one of the best friends you'll ever have. Treat him like a friend. (6) Keep an idea file or notebook. Never throw away your notes. Who knows when one of those ideas written on the back of a napkin will become a tremendous book? (7) Write every day. Write something. Force creativity. That's right. Waiting on 'inspiration' is bad business and a cop-out. Write a diary, if nothing else, or a commentary on your daily devotions. (8) Pray for enablement. Yes, pray, if you're going to write for a religious market. Ask God for divine insight.''

Johnson also says: ''(9) Make sure that you request permission for all material not covered by fair usage. The standard rule in copyright circles is that fair use covers quotations of fifty words or less provided there is sufficient publication information listed. For poems that are not in public domain (including song poems) it is always best to gain written permission from the person or firm which owns the copyright. For extensive uses of prose from the same source, the writer should seek written permission from the owner of the copyright. This will save horrible headaches for the editorial team in the event the book is published. (10) Read widely. I've had fledgling authors explain to me that they seldom read. That's a mistake. Reading widens your horizons, gives you insight, and helps your vocabulary. It doesn't mean that you copy another author's style, either. I'm a combination of all the people I've read. I pride myself on being a consummate author. No ego intended. I'm also a cognate of Charles Allen, Art Buchwald, Erma Bombeck, Eric Hoffer . . . Arthur Miller, Frank Baum, and James Baldwin. I owe a debt to all of them—and to thousands of others.''

Martha Perry of Liguori Books notes that some publishers, Liguori included, do very well with self-help books. She says, ''We have seen an upsurge in inspirational books based on true-life experiences. Overcoming a handicap against great odds makes for exciting and interesting reading, as long as the writer avoids the tone of maudlin sentimentality. Heroes and heroines are not cloying, sickeningly sweet people; and they become larger than life through their handling of difficult situations. Another form of publication that will always have an audience would be the presentation of down-to-earth ideas and suggestions of how to cope with some of life's problems. Human nature being what it is, these annoying little (or large) bugaboos will continue to plague us. Everyone gains some measure of satisfaction from hearing their problem is not insurmountable and that there just might be a very practical solution that they have not thought of or tried.''

Ms. Perry encourages beginning writers to keep trying to come up with significant ideas and manuscripts. ''The main thought an aspiring writer should keep in mind is to persevere. Just because one publisher does not like or cannot market the author's material is no basis for assuming that the material is unpublishable. Any constructive criticism offered by various editors should be weighed and implemented if possible; this is a good learning experience. Readers enjoy a well-written, interesting story—just because the story is true (and religious or spiritual) it need not be dry and dull. Write with enthusiasm and it will come over in the writing.''

Keith M. Bailey, formerly of Christian Publications, reminds authors, ''The most popular kind of nonfiction religious book today is the 'how-to-do-it' book dealing with practical aspects of the Christian life, family life, life style, or that category of books that deal with the how-to-do-it of ministry in the local church—evangelism, discipleship, and other forms of outreach ministry. There is still a good market for well-written devotional material.''

Mr. Bailey offers beginning authors the following general advice concerning topics and writing methods. ''First, they should give careful attention to their research. Make sure their material is credible, and, if they are quoting, that it is well documented. They should carefully proof their manuscripts discovering errors in grammar and punctuation. They should do at least three revisions and rewrites before submitting it to any publisher. Many beginning authors in their anxiety to publish, submit material before it is really polished and has the attractiveness it should have to appeal to an editor.''

Further, ''New authors should not attempt to invent new styles, but should work hard at becoming true craftsmen in the writing trade. There may be a few born geniuses among writers, but most good writers are the product of diligent and hard work in writing and rewriting. A new writer should make a goal to learn to be precise in stating material. One glaring weakness of many new writers is the lack of precision and consistency in the language used. Terms change meaning from chapter to chapter, leading the reader to utter confusion.''

Harvest House President, Robert H. Hawkins, agrees that ''how-to'' books are some of the best selling books for Christian publishers. Further, ''Human interest stories are generally not the type of books that sell unless the author is speaking to 1000 or more people every week. The book that is on a subject that is of vital interest to masses of people is the one that really sells.''

Philip Rawley, recently at Moody, urges new writers to read both widely and well: ''Reading good writing is great training for writing well.''

Multnomah's John Sloan advises aspiring authors to attend as many writers' conferences as possible. He also suggests that anyone wanting to write should read widely, both to help in his illustrative use of material in writing and in building vocabulary skills. Mr. Sloan suggests further that writers begin by working on magazine pieces before venturing into the book field.

Nelson's trade editor, Bruce Nygren, notes, ''Any well-written, creative book on almost any subject will always draw attention and may sell well.'' Included in this list are books on the home and family, prophecy, Bible exegesis, linked meaningfully to everyday life, high-interest biography, and one-of-a-kind specialities. As far as general advice, Mr. Nygren says, ''Don't shortcut study and practice in the mechanics of effective writing. Become a 'good writer' first, then go on to becoming a 'good Christian writer'.''

Wrap Up

As you can see from the comments of the editors above, each is different. Each represents a different style and philosophy of publishing religious books. From these words of advice, you, as an aspiring author, should realize that you really have your work cut out for you. However, do not be intimidated. You can, through study and discipline, write and get published.

As you "flesh out" your outline, and deal with the actual heart of your book, keep the comments of these experienced editors in mind. You might avoid having your work turned down by one of them.

Chapter 6

THE PUBLISHING CONTRACT: WHAT DOES IT ALL MEAN?

THE PUBLISHING CONTRACT: WHAT DOES IT ALL MEAN?

You have written your sample chapters, contacted a publisher, and are camping out by your mailbox. One day the postman brings a strange looking document entitled "Letter of Agreement." Only after you read the thing four times do you realize it's a contract from the editor offering to publish your book. But now what?

The first thing *not* to do is run out and buy a Cadillac. Yes, you will probably make some money from your book, but not enough for a new car. Three professors at Columbia University made a recent survey of 2,239 authors. They found that the average author earned $4,774 per year. Only 10 percent made incomes of $45,000 or above, and only 5 percent made $80,000 or more.[1] These are revealing statistics that you must heed, not to get discouraged, but to be realistic.

By 1985 religious book sales in the United States should reach well beyond $400 million.[2] You want your share of that total, but in all probability your share will be fairly small. Your rewards for writing will be something higher than just money. As Harry Emerson Fosdick once said, "Across the years one of the most gratifying rewards of my ministry has been the stream of letters, often from out-of-the-way places all over the world, bearing messages of appreciation for help received from those earlier books of mine."[3] This is an all-important perspective to keep on your writing ministry. After all, anyone can make money, but not everyone can make a positive, lasting contribution to another's life.

Back to contracts. What you must do, instead of planning to spend your future earnings at this point, is to try to understand the nature of the publishing contract. It is simply the written record of an agreement, agreed to and signed by the author and the publishing company. Contracts deal with future uncertainty by "providing advance solutions for different, predictable eventualities. They say, 'Here's what I'll do, and here's what you'll do, if your book needs revising, or sells 1,000,000 copies, or someone sues us, or any number of other events occur'."[4] There is no assurance that even when a publisher commits time and money to a publishing project that there will ever be a return of investment. Writing and publishing a book is a "gamble" for both the author and the publisher. Therefore, one way to look at the publishing contract is as " . . . an imperfect attempt at a fair division of the cost of losing and the rewards of winning."[5]

If a religious publisher offers to publish your book, the contract offered you will no doubt agree to have the publisher pay all printing and production costs, and to pay you specified royalties, among certain other standard matters. But remember, not every contract is alike. Here we want to alert you to those areas on which you should concentrate. If you are offered a contract, the first thing to do is to read it especially carefully. Talk to a lawyer knowledgeable in literary law about it if you have any reservation.[6]

We are not lawyers, nor experts on contracts, but we have seen our share of publishing agreements. Book publishing follows predictable patterns, and most of the publishing contracts you will come across will be fairly standard. (An example of one standard publishing agreement can be seen in Sample B.) This is not to say that even standard contracts can't be modified. They can. Most publishers are very used to making changes in the contract. You the author should be aware of the more typical contract provisions as well as some of the variations which can be used. What we want to do in this chapter is to show you two actual contracts, one rather simple and the other more complex, and to give you a 'guided tour' through the more complicated one. *Please refer to the sample contracts at the end of this chapter.*

The Simple Letter of Agreement

The first contract is a one-page letter of agreement, like the one shown in Sample A at the end of the chapter. It is simple, easy to understand, and short. The author's name goes in the blank line on #1, and the name of the manuscript goes in the second line. #2 has to do with royalty payments. If a straight fee is agreed upon for the work under contract, then the line 2a is marked out and the fee is stipulated in 2b. Most publishers pay a royalty based on a percentage of the selling price of the book, but they sometimes buy a manuscript outright with a "flat" or "straight fee." This type of form is popular when publishers negotiate such a straight fee payment.

Numbers 3, 4, 5, and 6 of this agreement specify clearly who is responsible for what. The author simply signs the contract and returns it to the publisher. You will not see many agreements in publishing which take this form. We will spend more time on the more typical publishing contract.

The Standard Publishing Contract

The second contract we will examine is a much more complicated document. (Consult Sample B.)

#1 is a standard grant clause. The grant of rights clause allows the author to transfer some or all of the ownership of a work to a publisher, giving the publisher permission to publish the manuscript. This clause tells you all the things your publisher can do with the work once he buys it. It will define whether the grant of rights to the publisher is complete and exclusive, or is limited in one way or another. Most religious publishers will ask for the "sole and exclusive right to print, publish and sell" their edition of your book in the English language in North America.

#2 allows the publisher to copyright the book in its name.

Since all a publisher needs is the legal right to publish, and not necessarily ownership of the copyright itself, most do not mind if authors insist on having their books copyrighted in their names and not that of the publishing house. This is sometimes an area of negotiation between an author and a publisher. If the copyright is to be kept in the author's name (where the author's name appears on the copyright page), the license to publish the book is then transfered to the publisher. If the publisher copyrights the book in its own name, then certain provisions are usually made in the contract for the copyright to revert to the author after certain things occur, such as the book going out-of-print.

#4 is a warranties and indemnities clause which is actually a protection used by publishers to indemnify them against possible lawsuits. The author certifies that the work is original and not plagiarized. The author further promises the publisher that he or she has every legal right to enter into a publishing agreement, and in so doing they are not interfering with anyone else's rights. Should these promises be breached, the author agrees to pay the publisher for any loss. (cf. #26)

In #5 the author agrees not to try to publish another book which would compete with the sale or impair sales of the work refered to in the contract. If the contracted work anthologized sermons, for example, the author could not offer a condensed version of the anthology to another publisher.

The author agrees to secure any necessary grants of permission to quote copyrighted works in #6. The general rule is that permission must be granted for all material still under copyright (unless it falls under the "fair use" doctrine of the Copyright Act, which permits a small amount of copying of a protected work without obtaining permission of the copyright owner). Since it is the author who knows what he or she has borrowed, it is sensible that the permissions responsibility should rest with the author and not the publisher.

#7 stipulates that the author will read the galley proofs of the manuscript and return them promptly to the publisher. It also stipulates that the author will not try to make major changes in the manuscript at that time. The reason for this is that once the material is in galley proof form, it is expensive to make such corrections. Galleys, by the way, are the tentative layout of the material in page form, the proofs being drawn from uncorrected copy set in a single column, on which an author proofreads and marks any errors in the margins. The typesetter then goes back and makes any necessary corrections prior to page makeup.

The eighth clause spells out the deadline for delivery of the final copy of the manuscript to the publisher. Many publishers are not that rigorous about the manuscript delivery date. If an author has a legitimate reason for being late, usually all that is required is keeping the publishing house properly informed. But don't count on this in all cases. The delivery date is very important because the publisher can terminate the contract if an author fails to get the manuscript to the editor in time. And if any advance money has been paid, the publisher can demand that it be returned. Authors should realize that publishers themselves operate under strict deadlines, and the late delivery of manuscripts can cause problems with work schedules, the printing of catalogs and promotional pieces for the books, and with sales more generally. Most writers will admit that the deadline is a wonderful discipline, and they are thankful to get one.

The ninth clause is directly related to the preceeding one. It gives the publisher the right to terminate the contract should the author fail to deliver the manuscript within a specified period of time from the stated delivery date.

The author agrees in #10 to provide an index if the publisher wants one. This is often a matter of negotiation, too. The publisher can provide an index as easily as the author.

#11 gives the publisher the right to edit the work. This is extremely important since it indicates who has the last say about what appears in the book. It is entirely standard for a publisher's contract to insist on the house's right to change the written material to fit its own editorial style. If you as the author wish final editorial control of everything in your book, you must be very sure to amend the contract to say so. Such a position is highly impractical for all but a few well established writers, however. It is best that you require of your editor that he or she consult with you regarding all changes, including the change of title. This also can be added to the contract.

The twelfth clause tells the author when he can expect publication of the book once the manuscript is delivered in satisfactory condition. Usually an author can expect his finished book within 12 or 18 months after the manuscript has been approved, depending on the sort of editing, typesetting method, graphics and printing technology used by the publisher on the particular book project.

#13 is *the* crucial paragraph for many authors. A royalty is a payment made to the author in exchange for granting the publisher the right to publish and sell your book. Sometimes a publisher will offer an author a one-time payment for a work, and in this case there is no continuing royalty payment. But most book publishing operates with a continuing royalty arrangement which is calculated as a percentage of the publisher's income from the sale of the book. The royalty is calculated in different ways, and it is of utmost importance to understand what this portion of your contract says.

Some contracts stipulate a royalty rate of a certain percentage (usually 8 to 10 percent on a hardcover trade book) on the *net* sales of the book. This means that the royalty will be figured on what the publisher receives from bookstores, libraries, distributors, book clubs, and other places where the book is sold. Let's say a book retails for $15.95. The royalty rate is not based on that figure, however. It is based on the price given to outlets. A discount of 40 percent is common. This means that the author would receive a 10 percent royalty on $9.57 instead of the $15.95 list price. The difference is substantial.

Most publishers offer a basic royalty rate of the suggested *retail* price of a book, with rates for paperbacks commonly a bit lower than for hardcovers. Most seem to think this arrangement favors the author more than the one based on the net price.

Letters "a" through "m" of #13 in the sample contract spell out in detail what royalties will be paid under certain conditions. These stipulations are often found in standard contracts. Authors should pay far more attention to these adjustment provisions than they normally do. Remember, the matter of royalty percentage payment is as open to negotiation as anything else in a publishing contract.

#14 stipulates what subsidiary rights belong to the publisher. These are called "subsidiary rights" or "sub rights" because they are usually less important than the primary right you give the publisher to initially publish and sell your book. As you can see from the sample contract under section 14, sub rights include a wide variety of media, some of which could actually prove more valuable than the right to publish the book in traditional form. In most cases, you will not be too concerned about your nonfiction religious book being made into a movie!

Clauses 15 through 18 explain in greater detail other matters related to royalties and payments. Most contracts in book publishing provide for royalty accounts to be computed annually or semi-annually, with payments figured "less returns." Returns are those books a bookseller returns to the publisher for credit because they failed to sell. Returns certainly affect royalty payments to authors because a publisher does not want to pay royalty based on a large number of books originally shipped if a significant portion of unsold books will be returned a few months later. So most publishers have a "reserve against returns" clause, with the sort of wording you will see in #15. This allows the publisher to withhold part of the author's royalties for a specified period of time (since publishers only allow bookstores to return books for a specified period of time). A "reasonable reserve" in these matters is usually based on a return rate of 20 to 25 percent of the books shipped. Be sure you get this spelled out.

Clause #19 in the sample contract does not include any type of insurance on the part of the author. But things are changing.

Many publishers have long bought defamation and liability insurance for themselves, and a growing number are now providing similar protection for their authors. This arrangement is only a very recent addition to some publishing agreements.[7]

#22 is the "termination" or "remainder and out-of-print clause." This gives the publisher the prerogative of declaring the book out-of-print when the demand for the work "shall not . . . be sufficient to render its publication profitable." This usually means the work has failed to sell a stated number of copies within a stated period of time. At least this number *should* be stated in your contract. The author should ask the publisher to be specific in this area.

In virtually all publishing agreements, the author has the right to buy unsold copies of the book, before it is remaindered, along with the plates and negatives in some cases, if the author wishes. With this option, the author can then sell the book to another publisher, or self-publish it.

"Remaindering" is a way the publisher can sell a title for a fraction of what it is actually worth. This is always a last-ditch effort for the publisher, since books are remaindered only after the publisher has determined they can be sold no other way. Many publishers will allow an author to require that his book not be remaindered for a designated period of time after its publication. But all published books are subject to remaindering if in the long run they do not continue to sell.

In paragraph 23, the contract states how many complimentary copies of the finished book the author gets for personal use. Most contracts contain such a clause. The important thing here, though, is not the number of free copies the author is allowed (it's usually anywhere from five to 25), but the price at which the author can purchase additional copies of the book from the publisher. This "buy-back" option is important for many writers who lecture or otherwise offer their own books for sale to the public through their appearances. Usually the publisher will insist on paying a more limited royalty on buy-backs if the author wishes a more generous discount on the books he buys back for resale. Again, the discount is a matter for negotiation.

#24 is another key clause. It is understandable that a publisher who takes a chance on one book project by an author wants to tie that author to the house for a possible future project. This the publisher can do through two contract clauses, "the option clause"and "the right of first refusal clause."

The option clause is certainly the most forceful clause from the publisher's point of view. It requires the author to sell his or her next book to the same publisher on the same terms of the present contract. Under the option clause, the author may not submit any future book to another publisher until after the original publisher has made a publishing decision.

Perhaps a more reasonable clause, at least from the author's point of view, is the right of first refusal clause. In this type of agreement, the author has to allow the original publisher the "first chance" at the author's next book project. Sometimes the publisher asks that it also be given a second chance—to match a better deal given the author by another publishing firm. The terms of a right to first refusal clause, including the response time a publisher has to make a decision, are open to negotiation. Negotiation is not possible under an option clause.

As an author, you would be better off either to negotiate the removal of these clauses altogether, if you can, or to sign a right of first refusal clause with a short publisher's response time. We have heard of some writers who purposely keep a "terrible" manuscript around for the sole purpose of living up to the letter of the law in such a right of first refusal clause. They say they know it is so bad that no publisher could possibly want it. After offering the "terrible" manuscript to the original publisher upon the publication of a first book, they can then turn to other houses to negotiate other projects as they wish. This rarely happens in religious publishing!

The assignment clause in #25 is contained in all publishing contracts. It protects both the publisher and the author should either wish to transfer the contract rights to another party, which transfer of rights has to be in writing. Assignments can occur when an author designates that the income from a book be paid to a creditor, for example, or when a publishing company sells its book list to another publisher, or when the company itself goes out of business. Usually a publisher keeps the right to make assignments unilaterally, but when the author wishes to assign rights or royalties to a third party the publisher typically reserves the right to agree with the assignment for it to be valid.

#26 is related to #4. Both have to do with copyright infringements and possible legal action taken against the author or the publisher. What is important in this section is to see if it is the author or the publisher, or both equally, who takes the financial burden if someone makes a claim of infringement of copyright on the work. You as an author should ask for an infringement provision in your contract which limits your financial liability to claims considered by a court. Otherwise, you could be held liable by the publisher for legal costs involved in claims which are bogus. Often, a publisher will withhold royalty payments pending the outcome of a lawsuit. You need to know how much of the entire royalty is to be withheld, and for how long. Also find out if you are liable for any agreed amount in the event that a judgement is made for the claimant.

A promotion clause, such as in #28 in the sample contract, is typical of publishing contracts, though what is included in this section depends on the size and kind of publisher you deal with. Many larger, mostly secular houses, commit to large sums of money for publicity and advertising campaigns, including author tours, media appearances and bookstore signing parties. This is very rare in religious publishing, even for the larger houses which specialize in religious books. But all houses, large and small, will want to promote an author's work by using the author's name, photo and biographic summary. The typical publishing contract will give the publisher this right.

If there are some things you definitely would or would not

do in the publicity and promotion of your book, these should be spelled out in this section of the contract.

The "Law Applicable" or "Governing Law" clause of #29 can be a headache for an author who lives in one state while his or her publisher's office is in another state. What the clause means is that the author must agree to tackle whatever legal hassles ensue from the book in the publisher's state. The author cannot be sued in his own state since through this clause he agrees that jurisdiction over disputes will always be in the publisher's home state. Nothing can be done about a clause like this. Don't worry. Most authors are in the same boat.

This sample contract has a provision for other stipulations, which is what #32 is. It is added to the existing agreements already given and allows either party by mutual consent to add other matters which they wish to specify.

For Further Assistance

You may want other help in knowing what to look for in a contract. The periodical *The Writer* will send you an article by Irwin Karp entitled, "What the Writer Should Look For in His First Book Contract." The address of *The Writer* is listed in chapter 7.

Any contract you sign with a publisher is an important, formidable document which could have a serious impact on your future. Be careful. Check it out with someone who knows publishing or literary law. Good literary agents might be helpful here, too. While it pays to be cautious, remember that reputable publishers have no desire to "rip you off" or to create bad feelings between themselves and you. Publishers live off the output of writers, so the relationship between the publisher and the author must be a symbiotic one. Most publishers want to cultivate a good working relationship with an author because if that writer's books sell, the publisher will want more of them.

We hope you have your first contract *soon*.

Sample A

LETTER OF AGREEMENT

Mailing Address _____
City, State, Zip _____
Social Security Number _____

This agreement between _____,
(Name of Author)
party of the first part, and F. Bandersnatch, Inc., Publishers
of Mythos, Michigan, organized and doing business under the
laws of the State of Michigan, party of the second part,
witnesseth:

1. That, whereas, _____, is author-
   (Name of Author)
   ized to assign publication rights of the manuscript
   _____ and the distribution rights
   (Name of Manuscript)
   during the full term of copyright and all renewals thereof
   to the F. Bandersnatch Publishing Co.
2. Royalties:
   a. _____ percent (_____%) royalty will be
      paid on the gross sale of all books sold.
   b. $_____ shall be paid at the time of publication
      for the rights to publish the author's manuscript.
   c. The author will receive a 40% discount on all books
      purchased from F. Bandersnatch, Inc., on all orders for
      five (5) or more copies.
   d. No royalty shall be paid on books sold to the author
      at the 40% discount schedule.
   e. One hundred and fifty copies are royalty exempt for
      review and gift purposes. Also, no royalty shall be paid
      on any additional copies given away for the purpose of
      review or promotion or on copies damaged by fire or
      water, or on copies sold as "remainders" or at below
      cost.

3. F. Bandersnatch, Inc. will furnish two copies of the book to the author without charge.

4. If at any time the sale does not warrant the continuation of the title, F. Bandersnatch, Inc. shall have the right to "remainder" the remaining stock, royalty exempt. However, the author shall be given the right to purchase the balance of the stock at production costs.

5. F. Bandersnatch, Inc. will handle all the typesetting, layout, design, and printing of said publication in its catalogues, through bookstore promotions, in its periodicals as long as it seems feasible and practical.

6. F. Bandersnatch, Inc. understands that the manuscript is original and free of any copyright infringements. (The author should request a release for reprinting any long quotations from a copyrighted source.)

(Signature of Author) (Date)

(Representative of F. B.) (Date)

Sample B

PUBLISHING AGREEMENT
F. Bandersnatch, Inc., Publishers

AGREEMENT made this ____ day of ____ 19 ____, between F. Bandersnatch, Inc., Publishers of Mythos, Michigan, hereinafter called the PUBLISHER, and _____

_____

whose address is _____
and _____
whose address is _____
(herein referred to, whether one or more, as AUTHOR), being the proprietor(s) of a work provisionally entitled _____

_____

_____

(hereinafter referred to as the WORK).

Grant

1. In consideration of the stipulations and covenants of the respective parties hereto, the AUTHOR hereby grants to the PUBLISHER its successors and assigns, the sole and exclusive right to publish and sell, or license the publication and sale of the above work in book form throughout the world during the full term of copyright and all renewals and extensions thereof, including the subsidiary rights hereinafter specified.

Copyright

2. The PUBLISHER, at its discretion, will register copyright to the WORK within three (3) months of publication in its name in accordance with the requirements of the copyright law of the United States. The PUBLISHER will take reasonable care to affix the proper copyright notice to each copy of the WORK.

Amendment of Law

3. All references to copyright made in this agreement are subject to such amendment and change as may be enacted by the Congress of the United States of America or by any other

legal authority with regard to the present Copyright Act or by the adoption of any new Copyright Act.

Author's Guarantee

4. The AUTHOR certifies to the PUBLISHER that he is the sole author and proprietor of said work; that the work is original and does not infringe upon the statutory copyright or upon any common law right, proprietary right or any other right whatsoever; that it contains nothing of an objectionable or libelous character; that the work is not in violation of any right of privacy; and that he and/or his legal representative shall and will hold harmless and keep indemnified the PUBLISHER from all suits and all manner of claims, proceedings and expenses, including attorney's fees, which may be taken or incurred on the ground that said work is such a violation, or contains something objectionable or libelous or otherwise unlawful. The AUTHOR undertakes for himself, his heirs and assigns, to execute at any time, on request of the PUBLISHER, any document of documents to confirm or continue any of the rights defined herein. AUTHOR guarantees that WORK has not heretofore been published; that he is the sole and exclusive owner of the rights herein granted to the PUBLISHER; and that he has not heretofore assigned, pledged, or otherwise encumbered the same.

Competing Edition

5. The AUTHOR shall not, without the consent of the PUBLISHER, publish any abridged or other edition of said work or any book of similar or competing character tending to interfere with the sale of the work covered by this agreement.

Permissions

6. If copyright material from other sources is included in the work, the AUTHOR shall, at his own expense, obtain from the copyright owners or their representatives written permission for use of such material, and shall deliver such permissions at the time of delivery of the final manuscript.

Author Proofs

7. The AUTHOR agrees to read and correct the galley and page proofs and return them to the PUBLISHER in such time and manner as will not delay the printer, and to pay, as a charge against royalties, or, at the option of the PUBLISHER, in cash, the expense of any alterations or additions authorized by the AUTHOR (other than those due to printer's errors) in the proof in excess of ten percent (10%) of the cost of composition of the said work as originally supplied by the AUTHOR, but in no case shall the PUBLISHER share of this cost exceed fifty dollars ($50.00), except by mutual and express consent.

Delivery of final manuscript

8. The AUTHOR agrees to deliver into the hands of the PUBLISHER on or before the day of _____ 19_____ a final revised copy of the manuscript, legibly typewritten and satisfactory to the PUBLISHER in content and form and ready to print from, including all charts, drawings, designs, photographs, and illustrations which are referred to in the text and intended to be a part thereof suitable for use by the PUBLISHER in preparing copies for reproduction. In event the AUTHOR chooses not to deliver such charts, drawings, designs, photographs, and illustrations, the PUBLISHER may supply them, charging the cost thereof against and deducting it from any or all monies accruing to the AUTHOR under this and/or other agreements between the AUTHOR and the PUBLISHER.

The PUBLISHER may with the consent of the AUTHOR, supply charts, drawings, designs, photographs, and illustrations which in their opinion are necessary to the content, promotion, and distribution of said work, charging the cost thereof against and deducting it from any or all monies accruing to the AUTHOR under this and/or other agreements between the AUTHOR and the PUBLISHER, except the cost of engraving and printing.

The length of the manuscript shall be approximately _____ words, and shall contain the following kind and approximate number of illustrations: _____

Time Limit for Publication

9. If, within the time specified in paragraph 8, such manuscript and support material is not delivered, the PUBLISHER shall not be bound by the time limit of publication hereinafter provided for, and in the event the manuscript is not delivered within three (3) months after delivery date specified in Paragraph 8, the PUBLISHER shall have the right of election to continue this agreement in effect or to terminate it and to receive back from the AUTHOR any monies paid or expended hereunder.

Index

10. If the PUBLISHER requests, the AUTHOR agrees to supply within 15 days after final page proof of the text has been submitted by the PUBLISHER, an index in proper content and form and ready to set type therefrom. If the AUTHOR fails to do so the PUBLISHER may have one prepared and charge the cost thereof to the AUTHOR.

Editing

11. The text and illustrations of said WORK shall be subject to editing and revision by the PUBLISHER prior to first publication, or to any subsequent printing; provided, however, that such editing or revision shall not materially change the meaning, or materially alter the text of said WORK without the AUTHOR'S consent. Editing to correct infelicities of expression, misstatements of fact, misquotations, errors in grammar, sentence structure, and spelling, and editing to make the WORK conform to the PUBLISHER'S style of punctuation, capitalization, and like details, shall not be considered as material changes.

Publisher's Agreement to Publish

12. The PUBLISHER agrees to publish said WORK at its own expense, not later than eighteen (18) months from the date of receipt of satisfactory manuscript, unless specified otherwise in this agreement in such style, and at such price as the PUBLISHER shall determine as best suited to its success

(including special prepublication price, if any). It is understood that advertising, number and destination of free copies, and all details of manufacture and publication shall be in the exclusive control of the PUBLISHER, and the stock of plates and books shall be the property of the PUBLISHER.

Royalty

13. The PUBLISHER shall pay to the AUTHOR royalty as follows:

(a) Ten percent (10%) of the net sales on all copies of the regular trade edition (except as noted hereinafter) sold by the PUBLISHER within the United States of America (by *net sales* is meant gross receipts less discounts to the trade);

(b) Five percent (5%) of net sales of the paperback edition sold by the PUBLISHER within the United States of America (by *net sales* is meant gross receipts less discounts to the trade).

(c) When in its judgment it is necessary or advisable, the PUBLISHER is authorized to sell copies of the WORK at a discount of fifty percent (50%) or more. When copies are sold at discounts of fifty percent (50%) or more, a royalty of five percent (5%) of net sales shall be paid to the AUTHOR.

(d) When copies are sold by the PUBLISHER through mail order, coupon advertising, or radio or television advertising, the royalty shall be five percent (5%) of the amount received therefrom, excluding postage and other handling charges.

(e) For the purpose of keeping the WORK in print and in circulation as long as possible, the AUTHOR agrees that, after two (2) years from the date of first publication of the regular trade edition, if in any twelve (12)-month period the sales do not exceed two hundred and fifty (250) copies, the royalty shall be one-half of the prevailing rate.

(f) The PUBLISHER shall have the right to arrange for foreign editions of said work, paying the AUTHOR fifty percent (50%) of the net payments received by the PUBLISHER.

(g) The PUBLISHER shall have the right to make arrangements for sales of American edition copies of the WORK outside the continental limits of the United States and its dependencies, paying the AUTHOR on such sales a royalty of ten percent (10%) of the amount actually received by the PUBLISHER.

(h) On copies of any cheap edition published by another firm, for which the PUBLISHER shall have the exclusive right to arrange, the AUTHOR shall receive fifty percent (50%) of the amount received by the PUBLISHER. Royalties on any cheap edition issued by the PUBLISHER shall be fixed by agreement between the AUTHOR and the PUBLISHER.

(i) On copies of a textbook edition at a reduced suggested retail selling price issued for sale to educational institutions, a royalty of five percent (5%) of the textbook suggested retail selling price shall be paid to the AUTHOR.

(j) On bound copies sold from PUBLISHER'S stock to or through recognized book clubs, a royalty of five percent (5%) of the suggested retail selling price shall be paid to the AUTHOR, provided, however, in the case of copies sold through the PUBLISHER'S recognized book clubs for use as one of two or more books offered as a main selection, the royalty shall be one-half of the aforementioned royalty; and provided, further, in the case of copies used as bonus or introductory offers in the PUBLISHER'S recognized book clubs, no royalty shall be paid.

(k) The PUBLISHER shall have the exclusive right to make arrangements with recognized book clubs granting them permission to print special editions of the WORK. Compensation for such rights shall be divided equally between AUTHOR and PUBLISHER.

(l) On the sale of sheet stock from the American edition sold to a foreign publisher, the AUTHOR shall be compensated at the rate of ten percent (10%) of the net amount received by the PUBLISHER.

(m) No royalties shall be paid upon copies given to the AUTHOR, salesmen's samples, damaged copies, returned

copies, copies given away to publicize the WORK or to promote sales, or copies sold at or below manufacturing costs as
determined by the PUBLISHER.

Subsidiary Rights

14. The following shall be considered as subsidiary rights,
for the sale of which the PUBLISHER shall be solely responsible; serial rights before and after book publication; dramatic,
public reading and other nondramatic performing rights;
motion picture rights; translations, digests, abridgements, selections and anthologies; also mechanical, visual such as microfilm
and micropoint (other than motion picture), sound reproduc-
ing and recording rights (including but not limited to television and broadcasting, phonographic, wire, tape, video, and
electro video recordings other than motion pictures); lyric rights
and adaptions of said WORK for commercial use. The division of receipts from the sales of subsidiary rights shall be as
follows:

(a) Except as provided in (c) and (d) of section 13, fifty
percent (50%) to the AUTHOR and fifty percent (50%) to the
PUBLISHER.

(b) Dramatic and/or motion picture, television and
broadcasting rights, and adaptations for commercial use:
seventy-five percent (75%) to the AUTHOR and twenty-five
percent (25%) to the PUBLISHER of the amount received by
the PUBLISHER.

(c) The PUBLISHER is authorized to grant permission, at no charge and without paying royalty, for use of the
work, or selections therefrom, by recognized organizations for
the physically disabled.

Royalty Payments

15. Royalty accounts shall be computed annually to the first
(1) day of April of each year, and statements thereof shall be
rendered and the amount shown due thereby paid on or before
the thirtieth (30) day of the following June. However, if in
the opinion of the PUBLISHER, there is a risk of booksellers
returning for credit a substantial quantity of unsold copies of

the WORK the PUBLISHER may withhold a reasonable reserve with which to compensate for such returns.

First Royalty Statement

16. If the WORK shall have been on sale for a period of time shorter than three months as of April 1 of a given year, the first statement shall be postponed until the next succeeding April 1 for computation.

Accounts Due Publisher

17. The AUTHOR agrees that any account, bills, advances, or amounts of any nature that may be due the PUBLISHER by the AUTHOR, whether under this agreement or not, shall be chargeable against and may be deducted from any or all monies accruing to the AUTHOR under this and/or other agreements between the AUTHOR and the PUBLISHER.

Taxes on Royalties

18. It is mutually agreed that any taxes, domestic or foreign, which are or may be levied on the AUTHOR'S royalties, when paid by the PUBLISHER are proper charges against the royalty earnings due under this agreement, and may be withheld by the PUBLISHER.

Insurance

19. No insurance whatever need be effected by the PUBLISHER for the AUTHOR.

Properly Spacing Author's Books

20. For the purpose of orderly and systematically promoting the AUTHOR'S reputation and acceptance as a writer, the PUBLISHER agrees not to publish this WORK until six months shall have elapsed since publication of the AUTHOR'S next preceding book, whether the next preceding book was published by the PUBLISHER or not, and the AUTHOR agrees that he will not permit his succeeding book to be published until six months shall have elapsed after publication of this WORK, whether the next succeeding book be published by the PUBLISHER or not.

Unavoidable Delay

21. It is mutually agreed that neither the AUTHOR nor the PUBLISHER shall be held responsible for any delays which may be due to abnormal conditions existing in manufacturing, publishing, and distribution of books, including shortages in manufacturing facilities, personnel, and materials.

Termination

22. If at any time during the continuance of this agreement the demand for the WORK shall not, in the opinion of the PUBLISHER, be sufficient to render its publication profitable and it wishes to discontinue permanently the publication of said WORK, the AUTHOR shall have the right to buy from the PUBLISHER as an entirety all copies on hand at the cost of the manufacture and the stamps, electrotype plates and engravings of illustrations (if in existence) at actual cost to the PUBLISHER, including the composition. If the AUTHOR fails to exercise this option by paying for the same in cash within thirty (30) days after notice has been mailed to him by the PUBLISHER to his latest known address by registered mail, the PUBLISHER may destroy or dispose of the same as it sees fit without commission or percentage, and this agreement shall forthwith cease and terminate.

Author Copies

23. The PUBLISHER will furnish six (6) copies of the published WORK to the AUTHOR at no charge. Should the AUTHOR desire additional copies for personal use, they shall be supplied at forty percent (40%) discount from the suggested retail selling price, carriage additional.

Right of First Refusal

24. The AUTHOR grants the PUBLISHER the right of first refusal on his next work. The AUTHOR shall not offer the same to someone else on more favorable terms without first offering the same to PUBLISHER on the same terms. Such option shall be exercised within ninety (90) days after the receipt by the PUBLISHER of the complete and final manuscript;

provided, however, that in no case shall the PUBLISHER be obligated to accept or decline such manuscript earlier than ninety (90) days after the publication of the WORK covered by this agreement. Should the PUBLISHER decline the first manuscript so offered under the option, the AUTHOR is relieved of obligation for further submission.

Assignment

25. This agreement may be assigned but only in its entirety and shall be binding upon and inure to the benefit of the personal representatives and assigns of the AUTHOR and upon and to the successors and assigns of the PUBLISHER. No assignment shall be valid, as against the PUBLISHER, unless a copy or duplicate original of the same shall have been filed with the PUBLISHER.

Suits for Infringement of Copyright

26. If the copyright of the WORK is infringed, and if the parties proceed jointly, the expenses and recoveries, if any, shall be shared equally and if they do not proceed jointly, either party shall have the right to prosecute such action, and such party shall bear all the expenses thereof, and any recoveries shall belong to such party; and if such party shall not hold the record title of the copyright, the other party shall permit the action to be brought in his or its name.

Sums Due and Owing

27. Any sums due and owing from the AUTHOR to the PUBLISHER, whether or not arising out of this agreement, may be deducted from any sum due, or that may become due from the PUBLISHER to the AUTHOR pursuant to this agreement.

Author's Name, Likeness, etc.

28. In connection with the publication, advertising, and marketing of the WORK, PUBLISHER shall, without restriction, have the right to use, and allow others to use, AUTHOR'S name, signature, and likeness, and biographic material concerning AUTHOR.

Law Applicable

29. This agreement shall be interpreted according to the law of the State of _____ regardless of the places of its physical execution.

Modification

30. This agreement constitutes the complete understanding of the parties. No modification or waiver of any provision shall be valid unless in writing and signed by both parties. The waiver of a breach of any of the terms hereof or any default hereunder shall not be deemed a waiver of any subsequent breach or default, whether of the same or similar nature, and shall not in any way affect the other terms hereof.

Limitation of Agreement

31. This agreement shall not be binding upon either the PUBLISHER or the AUTHOR unless it is signed by all and delivered to the PUBLISHER within a period of forty-five (45) days from the date of this agreement.

Amendments

32. This contract contains a memorandum of all the agreements, expressed or implied, between the parties hereto, but may be amended at any time by mutual consent of the parties hereto, but only in writing, signed by both parties and affixed to this contract and made a part thereof.

The changes, alterations, interlineations, and deletions made in Paragraphs _____ of this contract, and the additional typed clauses numbered _____ were made and added before the execution hereof.

Notice provision: Any notice to be given hereunder shall be sent by registered or certified mail, return receipt requested, addressed to the parties at their respective addresses above given. Either party may designate a different address by notice so given.

IN WITNESS WHEREOF the parties have duly executed this agreement the day and year first above written.

_____   _____

Author's Signature   Publisher's Signature

NOTES

1. From a UP release, in *The Louisville Times*, June 15, 1981, p. A2.

2. Estimated publishers' net book sales for hardbound and paperbound religious books in 1982 was $368 million. *Publishers Weekly Yearbook: News, Analyses & Trends in the Book Industry* (New York: R.R. Bowker, 1983), p. 97.

3. Harry Emerson Fosdick, *The Living of These Days* (New York: Harper & Row, 1956), p. 135.

4. Brad Bunnin and Peter Beren, *Author Law & Strategies* (Berkeley,Ca.: Nolo Press, 1983), p.6.

5. Ibid.

6. Helpful guides for the working writer on the publishing contract are Ted Crawford, *The Writer's Legal Guide* (New York: Hawthorne Books, 1977) and Kirk Polking and Leonard S. Meranus, editors, *Law and the Writer* (Cincinnati, Ohio: Writer's Digest Books, 1978), but especially Brad Bunnin and Peter Beren, *Author Law & Strategies* (Berkeley, Ca.: Nolo Press, 1983), pp.5-52.

7. Stuart Speiser looks at publisher's liability insurance in "Insuring Authors: A New Proposal," in *Publishers Weekly*, May 7, 1982, p.26.

Chapter 7

TOOLS: KNOW WHAT IS AVAILABLE

TOOLS: KNOW WHAT IS AVAILABLE

One writer likened the reading of religious literature to being stoned to death with popcorn. That is an interesting image. Popcorn is light, fluffy and not very substantial. Religious literature probably got this reputation because some writers of such material thought all they had to do was to sit down and pound out whatever sounded sweet—things about the brotherhood of man and the Fatherhood of God, we suppose. There may be a small place for such writing, but that place is not in most religious books or articles, especially not the good ones.

How do you keep from serving up theological popcorn? You do it by researching your topic. Regardless of what you are writing about, you do not know all there is to know about it, nor will you ever know all there is to know about it, and you will benefit from doing a little homework. Research will add substance and perspective to your work. Remember, you are not a spider, spinning your web of words from only your own insides. A writer is more like a honey bee, taking a bit of pollen from this flower and then that one, and putting it all together to make its honey. Do some research. Make some honey.

Writer's Market Books

There are many books you will no doubt wish to own and use as tools in your writing profession. Let us introduce you to three of them. They are gold mines of information and marketing tips. They will not be resources for research into your various topics of interest, but are instead resources for the writing process and the selling of your writing.

The Writer's Handbook: This is a *must* for the beginning writer. The volume is published by The Writer, Inc., the people who also publish the monthly magazine *The Writer*. They are located at 8 Arlington Street, Boston, Massachusetts, 02116. The book is updated annually so the current market information can be included. The latest edition is edited by Sylvia K. Burack, and sells for $19.95. This may sound expensive, but it is well worth the price, especially when you have within its covers most of the things you need to know about the writing and selling of short stories, novels, articles, nonfiction books, confessionals, poetry, plays, material for juveniles, science fiction, book reviews, and much more.

The *Handbook* is divided into four sections: Backgrounding for writers, how to write, the editorial and business side of writing, and the various markets for writers. There are 100 chapters by best-selling authors like Sidney Sheldon, Stephen King, Ken Follett, John Jakes, Phyllis A. Whitney, Neil Simon and Joyce Carol Oates. Then there are 82 additional chapters of practical advice and instruction on writing techniques, literary agents, editors, copyright, manuscript preparation, and so on. Two thousand up-to-date listings of where to sell your material are included. The first section has chapters on matters pertaining to pre-writing themes. For example, some of the chapter titles are, "Making the most of your talent," "Should I be a writer?," "Six most-asked questions on writing," and "Following one's instincts." All of the articles are helpful to the novice who may be asking, "Do I really want to be a writer?"

The second section is for those who answer this latter question affirmatively. It deals with techniques for writing. Sample chapter headings are, "What makes a fiction writer?," "How to write a novel," "Leaving the reader satisfied," "Finding the right shape for your story," "Writing from research," "Four tests for a paragraph," "Titles that talk," "Checklist for a salable article," "Writing for the teenage market," "Writing for the inspirational and religious market," and "Writing a television play."

Section three has chapters on business issues such as, "Legal rights for writers," "The role of the literary agent today," and "Manuscript preparation and submission."

Part four lists markets for your work. The lists include such places as popular magazines of general interest, specialized magazines such as detective and mystery, science fiction and romance magazines. Poetry markets are included, as are organs to sell fillers and humor, religious materials, juvenile and young adult writing. A good selection of book publishers is offered as well. Virtually all writers have a keen interest in market lists.

In the list of book publishers, you will find the entries presented as shown in the following examples:

ABBEY PRESS—St. Meinrad, In. 47577. John T. Bettin, Editor. Nonfiction books on family relationships. Pays on royalty basis. Query with table of contents and writing samples.

ABINGDON PRESS—201 Eigth Avenue South, Nashville, Tn. 37202. Ronald P. Patterson, Editorial Director. Religious books, juveniles, college texts, general nonfiction. Query with outline and sample chapters.

AUGSBURG PUBLISHING HOUSE—426 South Fifth Street, Minneapolis, MN 55415. Roland Seboldt, Director of Book Development. Fiction and nonfiction on Christian themes; juveniles. Pays on royalty basis.

The entries give you the "who, what and where" of the publishing trade. All in all, this book is worth the money you will spend for it. Read its nearly 900 pages, study it, mark it up. This is a tool you will want to keep sharp.

Writer's Market: This is published annually by Writer's Digest Books, 9933 Alliance Road, Cincinnati, OH 45242. These are the people who publish the monthly magazine *Writer's Digest*.

The latest edition lists for about $19.00. *Writer's Market* differs from *The Writer's Handbook* in that the *Market* is almost exclusively market information. There are 4,000+ buyers of freelance writing, giving names, addresses, pay rates, editorial needs, plus a new section of computer software publishers looking for freelance material. Less than ten percent of the book is devoted to matters relating to writing. This reference specializes in the selling of writing.

The market listings under Book Publishing in *Writer's Market* contain fuller entries than those in *The Writer's Handbook*. More information is given which helps a writer better judge the market potential for his or her particular project. The three examples cited above appear as follows in this resource manual:

ABBEY PRESS—St. Meinrad, In. 47577. (812) 357-8011. Publisher: Keith McClellan, OSB. Publishes original paperbacks. Averages 8 titles/year. Pays definite royalty on net sales. Query with outline and sample chapter. Reports in three weeks. SASE. Nonfiction: "Primarily books aimed at married and family enrichment. The materials must be typed and readable and must show some promise for the author (good grammar, etc.)." Recent Nonfiction Titles: *Walk On in Peace*, by Dorothy Edgerton; *Building Family:An Act of Faith*, by Paul Connolly; and *The Challenge of Fatherhood*, by Hugh Stanley.

ABINGDON PRESS—201 8th Avenue, South, Box 801, Nashville, TN 37202. (615) 749-6403. Editorial Director: Ronald P. Patterson. Managing Editor: Robert Hill Jr. Editor/Professional Books: R. Donald Hardy. Senior Editor/Reference Resources: Carey J. Gifford. Editor of Lay Books: Mary Ruth Howes. Editor of Academic Books: Pierce S. Ellis Jr. Editor of Childrens Books: Ernestine Calhoun. Publishes paperback originals and reprints. Published 120 titles last year. Pays royalty. Query with outline and samples. Write for ms. preparation guide. Reports in six weeks. SASE. Nonfiction: Religious-lay and professional, children's books and academic texts. Length: 32-200 pages. Recent Nonfiction Titles: *Introduction to Old Testament Study*, by J. Hayes; *Contagious Congregation*, by G. Hunter (evangelism); and *If I Were Starting My Family Again*, by J. Drescher. Fiction: Juveniles only. Recent Fiction Titles: *A Sweetheart for Valentine*, by L. Balian (baby adopted by entire village); and *The Devil's Workshop*, by K. Marcuse (historical fiction about Johann Gutenberg). Tips: "A short, pithy book is ahead of the game. Long, rambling books are a luxury few can afford."

AUGSBURG PUBLISHING HOUSE—426 South 5th Street, Box 1209, Minneapolis, Mn. 55440. (612) 330-3432. Director, Book Department: Roland Seboldt. Publishes hardcover and paperback originals (95 percent) and paperback reprints (5 percent). Publishes 45 titles/year. Pays 10-15 percent royalty on retail price; offers variable advance. Simultaneous and photocopied submissions OK. Reports in 6 weeks. SASE. Nonfiction: Health, psychology, religion, self-help and textbooks. "We are looking for manuscripts that apply scientific knowledge and Christian faith to the needs of people as individuals, in groups and in society." Query or submit outline/synopsis and a sample chapter or submit complete ms. Recent Nonfiction Titles: *The Friendship Factor*, by Alan Loy McGinnis; *Adventure Inward*, by Morton T. Kelsey (Christian growth through personal journal writing); and *Stress/Unstress*, by Keith W. Sehnert, MD. Tips: "We are looking for good contemporary stories with a Christian theme for the young readers in age categories 8-11, 12-14, and 15 and up." Submit complete ms.

As you can see, the market listings for book publishers in this market digest are full and complete. You will know what publishers handle what kind of materials, what to send, and to whom it should be addressed.

The Religious Writers Marketplace: Written by William H. Gentz and originally published in 1980 by Running Press of 125 South 22nd Street, Philadelphia, PA 19103, is available late in 1984 in a revised 1985 edition for $17.95. As the title indicates, this book is a reference aid for the religious writer devoted to the exclusive listing of markets which publish religious materials. One section lists religious periodicals, another lists religious book publishers, and a third gives the markets for Jewish articles and books. There is a survey of more than 1500 publishers and publications, including information on independent organizations and church-sponsored publishing programs, as well as the important evangelical field.

The fifth chapter of the book is a useful list of various opportunities in religious publishing, such as curriculum writing, and writing for greeting card companies, bulletin publishers, music publishers, drama houses, syndicates, and religious radio and television.

Chapter 6 lists additional resources for the writer, such as Christian writer's guilds and fellowships, conferences and workshops, correspondence courses, and newsletters. This book is well indexed and very valuable to the religious writer.

You will end up spending more than $55 for these three books. But if you are serious about writing books, and other religious material, these resources will pay for themselves many times over. People serious about writing will understand that they need to build up their professional library with the better reference sources. Besides, as a good word carpenter, don't you want the finest tools?

Magazines

Two magazines to which you might want to subscribe are *The Writer* and *Writer's Digest*. *The Writer* was founded in Boston in 1887. Each issue has articles on the art and craft of writing, a market listing for specialized markets, and departments such as "Prize Offers," "The Writer's Library," "Letters to the Editor," and a section which updates the ever changing market situation. For examples, they would list which editor is moving to which publisher, what magazine is suspending publication, and so on. You can subscribe to *The Writer* for about $15 per year at The Writer, Inc., 8 Arlington Street, Boston, Ma. 02116.

Writer's Digest is more of a "popular" magazine in that it is more trendy. Each issue has articles by well known writers on special topics of concern to contemporary writers. Departments cover current trends and topics, the writer's bookshelf, New York and Los Angeles market updates, and a look at the writer's life. Columns in each issue are on nonfiction, fiction, poetry and photography. Published by Writer's Digest, 9933 Alliance Road, Cincinnati, Ohio 45242, this magazine was founded in 1920. Subscription rates are currently about $18 per year.

Other magazines and newsletters you will want to consider are these:

Christian Writer's Newsletter. Publisher William Gentz will send you information about this profitable resource if you write to him at 300 East 34th Street, New York, New York 10016.

The Christian Writer. Information on this publication can be obtained by writing the editor/publisher Thomas Noton at P.O. Box 5650, Lakeland, Florida 33803.

Cross & Quill. This newsletter is a publication of the Christian Writers Fellowship. Information on it can be had by writing the editor, Joan Unger, at 2548 Abigail Drive, Spring Hill, Florida 33526.

Currents. The Christian Writer's League of America publishes this newsletter. Its address is 1604 East Taylor Avenue, Harlingen, Texas 78550.

While not specifically related to Christian writing, the two following publications are nevertheless beneficial:

Coda: Poets & Writers Newsletter. This magazine is published by Poets & Writers, Inc., at 201 West 54th Street, New York, New York 10019.

Writer's Lifeline. Vesta Publications, Ltd. publishes this resource at P.O. Box 1641, Cornwall, Ontario K6H 5V6, Canada.

Drop a note to any of these publications requesting information. You might be pleasantly surprised to discover the large number of good resources available to help you in your ministry of writing.

Literary Market Place

Another tool with which you will want to acquaint yourself is the *Literary Market Place*. This one is a good resource to read in the library, unless you wish to purchase the paperback copy which sells for nearly $60. R.R. Bowker is the publisher, 205 East 42nd Street, New York, New York 10017.

This book is extremely valuable because of the absolute wealth of information it contains. For example, a recent edition is divided into 14 sections: (1) Book Publishing (2) Associations (3) Book Trade Events (4) Courses, Conferences and Contests (5) Agents and Agencies (6) Services and Suppliers (7) Direct Mail Promotion (8) Review, Selection and Reference (9) Radio, TV and Motion Pictures (10) Wholesale, Export and Import (11) Book Manufacturing (12) Book Manufacturing (classified by services offered) (13) Magazine and Newspaper Publishers (14) Names and Numbers.

Almost anything you might want to know about markets, publishers, agents, courses and conferences related to writing and publishing, and so on, are to be found in this extraordinary and exhaustive professional reference volume.

Conferences

An excellent resource for any writer, especially a beginning one, is a writers' conference and workshop. You may wish to attend one or more of the growing number of Christian writing conferences. Rubbing elbows with other authors and editors can give you insights and inspiration you would otherwise miss, and go a long way towards honing your writing skills. Listed below are only some of the many fine writing conferences. Check *The Religious Writers Marketplace* for a more detailed state-by-state listing, and follow the conference list made available by the *Christian Writers Newsletter.*

Akron Manuscript Club Writers Conference, University of Akron, Ohio, May. Write: Vivian M. Preston, 248 4th St. NW, Barberton, OH 44203.

Anderson College Writers' Conference, Anderson College, 316 Boulevard, Anderson, SC, July. Write: Robert L. Richardson at college address.

Beginning Christian Writers Workshop, Forest Falls, California, June. Write: Wes Hardy, Forest Home Christian Conference Center, Forest Falls, California 92399.

Biola University Writers' Conference, La Mirada, California, June. Write: Dr. Lowell Saunders, Biola University, 13800 Biola Ave., La Mirada, CA 90639.

Blue Ridge Christian Writers Conference, Black Mountain, North Carolina, July/August. Write: Yvonne Lehman, PO Box 188, Black Mountain, NC 28711.

Brite School of Christian Writing, Dallas/Fort Worth, Texas, May. Write: Verna Berry, 7517 Terry Court, Fort Worth, TX 76118.

Christian Writer's C. S. Lewis Workshop, Clear Lake, Iowa, April. Write: Marvin Ceynar, Box 308, Dumont, IA 50625.

Christian Writers' Grand Ole Workship, Nashville, Tennessee, July. Write: Dr. John Warren Steen, 6511 Currywood Drive, Nashville, TN 37205.

Christian Writers Institute Conference and Workshop, Wheaton, Illinois, June. Write: Becca Anderson, 396 St. Charles Rd., Wheaton, IL 60188.

Christian Writers' School, Otterburne, Manitoba, July. Write: Mrs. Sara Pasiciel, Winnipeg Bible College, Otterburne, Manitoba, Canada R0A 1G0.

The Christian Writers' Seminar, Lakeland, Florida. Write: Gary R. Gay, c/o *The Christian Writer,* P.O. Box 5650, Lakeland, Florida 33803. (Available for engagements in cities across U.S.)

Christian Writers Workshop, Berrien Springs, Michigan,

June. Write: Dr. Kermit Netteburg, Andrews University, Berrien Springs, Michigan 49104.

Communication Through the Written Word, Princeton, New Jersey, April. Write: Dr. Jack Cooper, Princeton Theological Seminary, Princeton, NJ 08540.

Decision School of Christian Writing, Minneapolis, Minnesota, August. Write: Lori J.P. Sorensen, Box 779, Minneapolis, MN 55440.

Full Gospel Nor-Cal Workshop, Yuba City, California, November. Write: Mrs. Lou Vaughn, 2032 Blevin Rd., Yuba City, CA 95991.

Forest Home School of Christian Writing, Forest Falls, California. Beginners—June. Others—October. Write: Wes Hardy, Forest Home Christian Conference Center, Forest Falls, CA 92339.

Free Will Baptist Writers' Conference, Nashville, Tennessee, May. Write: H. D. Harrison, Free Will Baptist College, Box 17306, Nashville, TN 37217.

Inspirational Romance Writers Conference, Black Mountain, North Carolina, August. Write: Yvonne Lehman, Box 188, Black Mountain, NC 28711.

Maranatha Christian Writers' Seminar, Muskegon, Michigan, June. Write: Sandra Aldrich, Maranatha Bible and Missionary Conference, Muskegon, MI 49441.

Mississippi Valley Writers' Conference, Rock Island, IL, June. Write: David R. Collins, 3403-45th St., Moline, IL 61265.

Mount Hermon Christian Writers Conference, Mount Hermon, California, April. Write: David R. Talbott, Box 413, Mount Hermon, CA 95041.

Nazarene Writers Conference, Olathe, Kansas, August. Write: Dr. J. Fred Parker, Box 527, Kansas City, MO 64141.

Nor-Cal Christian Writer's Workshop, Sacramento, California, August. Write: Darlene Bogle, 24361 Soto Rd. (#3), Hayward, CA 94544.

St. David's Christian Writers' Conference, St. David's,

Pennsylvania, June. Write: Gayle G. Roper, RD 6, Box 112, Coatesville, PA 19320.

Seattle Pacific Christian Writers Conference, Seattle, Washington, June. Write: Rose Reynoldson, Humanities Dept., Seattle Pacific University, Seattle, WA 98119.

Southwest Christian Writers Seminar, Farmington, New Mexico, September. Write: Patricia Burke, 3204 Coronado Ave., Farmington, NM 87401.

Warm Beach Writers Conference, Stanwood, Washington, October. Write: Rich Hay, Warm Beach Camp, 20800 Marine Dr., NW, Stanwood, WA 98292.

Warner Pacific College Christian Writers Conference, Portland, Oregon, March. Write: Dr. Dale W. Mark, Warner Pacific College, 2219 SE 68th, Portland, OR 97215.

Writer's Workshop (Southern Baptist), Nashville, Tennessee, July. Write: Bob Dean, PO Box 24001, Nashville, TN 37203.

Write to Publish Workshops, Chicago, Illinois. Unpublished authors, June; Published authors, separate workshop, June. Write: Carolyn Klingbell, Moody Bible Institute, 820 North La Salle Dr., Chicago, IL 60610.

Writing for Publication Workshops, Pittsburgh, Pennsylvania, April/May. Write: Continuing Education Office, Pittsburgh Theol. Seminary, Pittsburgh, PA 15206. Richmond, Virginia, July. Write: PSCE, 1205 Palmyra Ave., Richmond, VA 23227.

Libraries

Once you have reflected on the art of writing, and have in mind a tentative idea about a publisher, you will be ready to begin serious research on your chosen topic. The obvious place to begin such research is your local library. [You might also write to the General Theological Library of 14 Beacon Street, Boston, Ma. 02108, to receive their quarterly bulletin of religious books which can be borrowed by mail anywhere in the United States.]

Go to the Card Catalog and use the Subject Guide first. If, for example, you are writing a book on the positive effects of religious practices in the home, look at the cards under "Family." Depending on the holdings of that library, you might find many books specifically on religion and the family, or you might find few or none. Let your mind wander and freely associate. What else might your topic be listed under? Try "Religion" to see if there might be books on religion and the home. Use whatever key words you might have on your subject. In this case, "Home," "Family," and "Religious Practices" are but three such.

Peruse the books you find listed in the card catalog. Some will pertain directly to your topic, some will be of marginal value, and others will be of no use to you at all. Another way to find books is to browse through the shelves. To do this you need to know the general classification of your topic in the Dewey Decimal Classification. The example listed above, on religion in the home, is listed in the 249s in the Dewey Decimal System of classification. Find that area in the library and see what is available. Some libraries have closed shelves which means that only an employee can get the books. This unfortunate system makes shelf browsing almost impossible.

If you are going to do any serious research in a library, you must have a working understanding of the Dewey Decimal System of Classification of books. Included below is a general summary of this system, and also the more detailed sub-classification for religion.

DEWEY DECIMAL CLASSIFICATION
GENERAL SUMMARY

000 GENERAL WORKS
010 Bibliography
020 Library Science
030 General Encyclopedias
040 General Collected Essays
050 General Periodicals
060 General Societies
070 Newspapers Journalism
080 Collected Works
090 Manuscripts & Rare Books
100 PHILOSOPHY
110 Metaphysics
120 Metaphysical Theories
130 Branches of Psychology
140 Philosophical Topics
150 General Psychology
160 Logic
170 Ethics
180 Ancient & Medieval Philosophy
190 Modern Philosophy
200 RELIGION
210 Natural Theology
220 Bible
230 Doctrinal Theology
240 Devotional & Practical
250 Pastoral Theology
260 Christian Church
270 Christian Church History
280 Christian Churches & Sects
290 Other Religions
300 SOCIAL SCIENCES
310 Statistics
320 Political Science
330 Economics
340 Law
350 Public Administration
360 Social Welfare
370 Education
380 Public Services & Utilities
390 Customs & Folklore
400 LANGUAGE
410 Comparative
420 English
430 German
440 French
450 Italian
460 Spanish
470 Latin
480 Greek
490 Other Languages

500 PURE SCIENCE
510 Mathematics
520 Astronomy
530 Physics
540 Chemistry
550 Earth Sciences
560 Paleontology
570 Anthropology & Biology
580 Botanical Sciences
590 Zoological Sciences
600 TECHNOLOGY
610 Medical Sciences
620 Engineering
630 Agriculture
640 Home Economics
650 Business
660 Chemical Technology
670 Manufactures
680 Other Manufactures
690 Building Construction
700 THE ARTS
710 Landscape & Civic Art
720 Architecture
730 Sculpture
740 Drawing & Decorative Arts
750 Painting
760 Engraving
770 Photography
780 Music
790 Recreation
800 LITERATURE
810 American
820 English
830 German
840 French
850 Italian
860 Spanish
870 Latin
880 Greek
890 Other Literature
900 HISTORY
910 Geography, Travel & Description
920 Biography
930 Ancient History
940 Europe
950 Asia
960 Africa
970 North America
980 South America
990 Pacific Islands

DEWEY DECIMAL CLASSIFICATION
RELIGION

200 RELIGION
201 Philosophy & Theories
202 Handbooks & Outlines
203 Dictionaries & Encyclopedias
204 Essays & Lectures
205 Periodicals
206 Organizations & Societies
207 Study & Teaching
208 Collections
209 History
210 NATURAL THEOLOGY
211 Knowledge of God
212 Pantheism
213 Creation of Universe
214 Theodicy
215 Religion & Science
216 Good & Evil
217 Worship
218 Immortality
219 Analogy

220 BIBLE
221 Old Testament
222 Historical Books
223 Poetic Books
224 Prophetic Books
225 New Testament
226 Gospels & Acts
227 Epistles
228 Revelation
229 Apocrypha
230 DOCTRINAL THEOLOGY
231 God
232 Christology
233 Man
234 Salvation
235 Angels, Devils, Satan
236 Eschatology
237 Future State
238 Christian Creeds
239 Apologetics

240 DEVOTIONAL & PRACTICAL
241 Moral Theology
242 Meditations
243 Evangelistic Writings
244 Miscellany
245 Hymnology
246 Christian Symbolism
247 Sacred Furniture & Vestments
248 Personal Religion
249 Family Worship

250 PASTORAL THEOLOGY
251 Preaching (Homiletics)
252 Sermons
253 Pastor
254 Church & Parish Administration
255 Brotherhoods & Sisterhoods
256 Societies for Parish Work
257 Parish Education Work
258 Parish Welfare Work
259 Other Parish Work
260 CHRISTIAN CHURCH
261 Christian Social Theology
262 Government & Organization
263 Sabbath, Lord's Day, & Sunday
264 Public Worship, Ritual & Liturgy
265 Sacraments & Ordinances
266 Missions
267 Religious Associations
268 Religious Education & Sunday Schools
269 Revivals & Spiritual Renewal
270 CHRISTIAN CHURCH HISTORY
271 Religious Orders
272 Persecutions
273 Heresies
274 In Europe
275 In Asia
276 In Africa
277 In North America
278 In South America
279 In Other Parts of the World
280 CHRISTIAN CHURCHES & SECTS
281 Primitive & Oriental Churches
282 Roman Catholic Church
283 Anglican Churches
284 Protestantism
285 Presbyterian & Congregational Churches
286 Baptist & Immersionist Churches
287 Methodist Churches
288 Unitarian Church
289 Other Christian Sects
290 OTHER RELIGIONS
291 Comparative Religion
292 Greek & Roman
293 Teutonic & Norse Religions
294 Brahmanism & Buddhism
295 Zorastrianism & Related
296 Judaism
297 Islam & Bahaism
298
299 Other Non-Christian Religions

Some libraries use the Library of Congress system because it is capable of being divided into minute categories, and is easily expandable. The general outline of this system is as follows:

A General Work—Polygraphy
B Philosophy—Religion
C History—Auxiliary Sciences
D History and Topography (except America)
E-F America
G Geography—Anthropology
H Social Sciences
J Political Science
K Law
L Education
M Music
N Fine Arts
P Language and Literature
Q Science
R Medicine
S Agriculture—Plant and Animal Husbandry
T Technology
U Military Science
V Naval Science
Z Bibliography and Library Science

While you will want to consult books on your subject, you will also need to read articles in magazines and journals. It is possible that a book can be somewhat dated before it is even released from the press, but periodical articles are usually more timely and fresh. We are fortunate today that so many different indexes are available to help us find exactly what we are looking for in journal and magazine sources. Listed below are some of the better indexes you will want to consider using in your research.

Access—indexes about 160 general magazines and has a good listing of city and regional magazines.

Art Index
Applied Science and Technology Index
Biography Index
Book Review Digest
Book Review Index
Business Periodicals Index
Catholic Periodical and Literature Index
Christian Periodical Index
Consumer Index to Product Evaluations and Information Sources
Cumulative Index to Periodical Literature
Dissertation Abstracts
Education Index
Film Literature Index
Guide to Social Science and Religion in Periodical Literature
Guide to the Performing Arts
Historical Abstracts
Humanities Index
An Index to Book Reviews in the Humanities
Index to Free Periodicals
Index to How-to-Do-It Information
Index to Jewish Periodicals
Index to New England Periodicals
Index to Periodical Articles By and About Blacks
Magazine Index—lists about 370 magazines, but is available only on microfilm.
New Periodicals Index
The New Review of Books and Religion
New Testament Abstracts
New York Times Index
Old Testament Abstracts
Pastoral Care and Counseling Abstracts
The Philosopher's Index
Physical Education Index
Physical Education/Sports Index
Popular Periodicals Index
Psychological Abstracts

Reader's Guide to Periodical Literature
Religion Index One: Periodicals—prior to 1979 this index was
    known as *Index to Religious Periodical Literature*
Religious and Theological Abstracts
The Review of Books and Religion
Science of Religion Abstracts and Index of Recent Articles
Sociological Abstracts
Southern Baptist Periodical Index
Subject Index to Children's Magazines
The United Methodist Periodical Index

Many other indexes exist, but these will certainly be
instrumental in assisting your quest for vital information in
your research and writing work.

An unidentified news correspondent once wrote,

> Some men die of shrapnel
> Some go down in flames.
> But most men perish inch by inch
> Who play at little games.[1]

Writing, like men, can perish inch by inch, and so can the
writer! Do not write if you intend to "play at little games."
Remember the analogy of religious literature being like popcorn (or in many cases, just plain corn). Do your homework.
Research your topic. Ask what others can teach you about it.
Remember God's words to Aaron in Numbers 18:29: "Give
it from the *best* that you receive."

NOTE

1. Cited by Floyd Thatcher in *The Religious Writers Marketplace*, by
William H. Gentz and Elaine W. Colvin (Philadelphia, PA: Running Press,
1980), p. xiv.

Chapter 8

MARKETS: WHERE TO SELL YOUR BOOKS

MARKETS: WHERE TO SELL YOUR BOOKS

If you are anything like most writers we have known, you have been biting at the bits to get to this chapter (or maybe you are fudging and reading this one first). In either case, you are correct in realizing that you need to understand book markets in order to find a place for your work.

One of the things you need to be conscientious about is to scout out any publisher which might possibly have an interest in the kind of book on which you are working. Read magazines like *Christianity Today*, *Eternity*, and *Moody Monthly* to see which publishers advertise there. What do they advertise? What topics seem to be current? Do some of the publishers seem to specialize in particular books? Who are some of the top-selling authors? Look at their books, not to copy their style, but to get an idea of how they communicate.

Write to various publishing companies and request copies of their catalogs and authors' guidelines. Most have free catalogs they will be happy to send. (It is assumed that you will *always* include with your correspondence a SASE.) Get to know the editors of these houses; they are your entrance into the world of print.

In compiling our list of most of the better book markets, we corresponded with every firm mentioned here and have had personal replies from all of them. We also talked with some over the phone, or personally at book meetings. We have even sold books to some of them. Others have sent nice, neat xeroxed form letters. These editors and publishers are not included in this chapter. We cannot guarantee that all the editors listed will respond to you as they did us. But so far as we know, these people enjoy being treated as human beings and will respond accordingly. Give them a try. Tell them what your projects are. One thing to keep in mind is this—query only one at a time. You don't want to sell your book to two or three publishers at the same time. Unforgivable!

ABINGDON PRESS

201 Eighth Avenue, South
Nashville, Tennessee 37202
(615) 749-6459

Meredith Carr, Managing Editor

Abingdon is a publishing arm of the United Methodist Church. The house handles religious books such as Bible studies, minister's aids, professional and academic texts, as well as some children's materials. Submit a prospectus.

ACCENT PUBLICATIONS, INC.

12100 West Sixth Avenue
(P.O. Box 15337)
Denver, Colorado 80215
(303) 988-5300

Jerry A. Wilke, Executive Editor

Accent publishes evangelical Christian books in the self-help field, family relationships, personal growth and fulfillment, money management, and so on. The house also publishes a significant amount of curriculum material for Sunday School and vacation Bible schools. Send manuscript with SASE.

ALBA HOUSE

2187 Victory Boulevard
Staten Island, New York 10314
(212) 761-0047

Anthony Chenevey, Editor-in-Chief

This is a Catholic publishing house which publishes devotional material, Bible study helps, and biographies. Send a query letter with SASE.

ALNUTT PUBLISHING
3029 South Olympia Circle
P.O.Box 879
Evergreen, Colorado 80439
(303) 670-3390

Frank Alnutt, President

This new company is looking for books which will have appeal in both the Christian and secular arenas. The material must apply Christianity in some way. A query letter with a book outline and a single sample chapter should be sent.

ALPINE PUBLICATIONS
1901 South Garfield Street
Loveland, Colorado 80537

Betty Jo McKinney, Publisher

This publisher deals with books for working women. Send a query with SASE.

ARBUTA HOUSE
P.O. Box 48
Abington, Pennsylvania 19001

V. Kerry Inman, President

Arbuta House publishes Bible study material which can be used in adult Sunday Schools. They do joint publishing to which the author contributes about $1,500.00.

ARGUS COMMUNICATIONS
P.O. Box 7000
Allen, Texas 75002
(214) 727-3346

Jim Porst, Vice President, Trade Division

Argus produces books for high school and adult lay audiences, including devotions and more psychological works. Send a sample of no more than two chapters, along with a cover letter.

AUGSBURG PUBLISHING HOUSE
426 South 5th Street
P.O. Box 1209
Minneapolis, Minnesota 55440
(612) 330-3300

Roland Seboldt, Director of Book Development

Augsburg, affiliated with the American Lutheran Church, publishes reference books, theology, Bible studies, books on various social concerns, and inspirational/devotional works for children and adults. They ask for a query letter with sample chapters.

BAKER BOOK HOUSE
P.O. Box 6287
Grand Rapids, Michigan 49506
(616) 676-9186

Daniel Van't Kerkhoff, Editor

Baker is a major evangelical house which produces works for both lay and academic audiences. Their interest is broad and varied, and includes ministers' worship aids, theology, history, devotions, and biographies. Manuscripts may be sent with SASE.

BEACON HILL PRESS (see NAZARENE PUBLISHING HOUSE)

BEACON PRESS
25 Beacon Street
Boston, Massachusetts 02108
(617) 742-2110

Marie Cantlon, Senior Editor

A publishing arm of the Unitarian Universalist Association, Beacon publishes controversial and liberal books addressed at exploring the human condition in the categories of general nonfiction, religion, psychology, philosophy and world affairs. Query letter with outline and/or table of contents should be sent. Sample chapters are preferred over complete manuscripts.

BETHANY HOUSE PUBLISHERS
(BETHANY FELLOWSHIP)
6820 Auto Club Road
Minneapolis, Minnesota 55438
(612) 944-2121

Carol A. Johnson, Managing Editor
Nathan Unseth, Assistant Editor

Bethany publishes books for a broad range of Christian readers, including children and adults. They use human interest stories of God at work among people, Bible study tools, and some inspiration. Send query letter, chapter by chapter synopsis, and a couple of finished chapters as samples.

THE BETHANY PRESS (see **CBP PRESS**)

BRANDEN PRESS, INC.
21 Station Street
Box 843
Brookline Village, Boston, Massachusetts 02147
(617) 734-2045

B.J. Levin, Editor-in-Chief

Branden publishes several religious books each year on Eastern and African religions related to Christianity. They consider other types of books which bring authenticity to characters and situations. Query letter only for nonfiction works.

THE BRETHREN PRESS
1451 Dundee Avenue
Elgin, Illinois 60120
(312) 742-5100

Leslie R. Keylock, Editor

The Brethren Press publishes books on a wide variety of topics of interest to the Christian community, including both popular and more academic works. The Press wishes to work closely with writers in the development of projects, and therefore suggests prospective authors send an idea synopsis of the book in the early stages of writing.

BROADMAN PRESS
127 Ninth Avenue, North
Nashville, Tennessee 37234
(615) 251-2000

Joe S. Johnson, Editor of Inspirational Books
Thomas L. Clark, Supervisor of Books and Music

Broadman is the publishing arm of the Sunday School Board of the Southern Baptist Convention, but you do not need to be a Baptist to publish with them. They produce books of devotional reading, reference works, Bible studies, sermons, etc., for both scholars and laity. They need to see a well-written synopsis, an outline of the whole project, and two or three sample chapters, though they do accept manuscripts.

CBP PRESS
P.O. Box 179
St. Louis, Missouri 63166
(314) 371-6900

Herbert Lambert, Editor

Formerly **THE BETHANY PRESS**, CBP (Christian Board of Publications) is related to the Disciples of Christ. They seek materials of mainline Protestant interest, and especially books on Christian unity. The trade books area here will receive a wider platform. Manuscripts are accepted with SASE.

C.S.S. PUBLISHING COMPANY
628 South Main
Lima, Ohio 45804
(419) 227-1818

Michael Sherer, Editorial Director

This publisher puts out books on creative topics relating to the Christian faith. This includes sermons, worship aids, Bible studies, devotions, materials for Sunday Schools, retreats and evangelism. They also publish dramas. While most of their materials are for the clergy, they are slowly expanding to the lay Christian market. This house prefers that writers send full manuscripts.

CATHOLIC UNIVERSITY OF AMERICA PRESS
620 Michigan Avenue, N.E.
Washington, D.C. 20064
(202) 635-5052

David McGonagle, Director

This university press publishes books for scholars and the academic community. Most of the titles are specifically for Roman Catholics. Send a query letter and a two-page summary abstract.

CHARIOT BOOKS
850 North Grove Avenue
Elgin, Illinois 60120
(312) 741-2400

Cathy Davis, Managing Editor

This division of **DAVID C. COOK PUBLISHING COMPANY** publishes childrens books which teach readers about the Bible in fun and interesting ways. They also do books to help children understand their feelings and problems, books about sports, science, animals, true stories, fiction, and "making choices" books. No unsolicited manuscripts.

CHOSEN BOOKS
Route 723
Lincoln, Virginia 22078
(703) 338-4131

David M. Hazard, Editorial Manager

Chosen Books is interested in presenting a Christian worldview to Christian and secular readers through biographies, testimony books, some novels, and teaching materials. All must emphasize the evangelical approach to Christianity. Send a query letter with synopsis and/or outline.

CHRISTIAN CLASSICS
Box 30
Westminster, Maryland 21157
(301) 848-3065

John J. McHale, Director of the Press

Christian Classics produces mostly Catholic books of theology, spirituality, reference, biography and history. Their subjects also include psychology and general nonfiction religious materials. They appreciate the query approach.

CHRISTIAN EDUCATION PUBLISHERS
7348 Trade Street
San Diego, California 92121
(619) 578-4700

Frank Hardman, Editor

Formerly called **SUCCESS WITH YOUTH PUBLICATIONS**, this firm is looking for childrens and youth-club curriculum. Send query letters.

CHRISTIAN PUBLICATIONS
3825 Hartzdale Drive
Camp Hill, Pennsylvania 17011
(717) 761-7044

Robert Cowles, Executive Vice President

This publisher is interested in Bible studies and books related to evangelical faith in a work-a-day world. They prefer authors send full manuscripts.

CONCORDIA PUBLISHING HOUSE
3558 South Jefferson Avenue
St. Louis, Missouri 63118-3968
(314) 664-7000

Jaroslav J. Vajda, Editor, Devotional/Inspirational Books
Mervin Marquardt, Editor, Childrens Books
William T. Simmons, Editor, Professional Books

Concordia is the publishing arm of the Lutheran Church-Missouri Synod. It publishes well-researched books on religion in keeping with the teaching of the Lutheran Church. Send query letter, sample chapter and table of contents of the writing project.

DAVID C. COOK PUBLISHING COMPANY
850 North Grove Avenue
Elgin, Illinois 60120
(312) 741-2400

Marlene LeFever, Director of Ministry Resources

David C. Cook publishes reference books, Bible studies, devotions, and Sunday School curriculum for youth and adults, laypersons and scholars. Query letters only for initial contact.

THE CONTINUUM PUBLISHING CORPORATION
575 Lexington Avenue
New York, New York 10022
(212) 532-3650

J. George Lawler, Senior Editor
Current affairs, social and educational concerns, psychology,
religion, sociology, history, self-help and biography. Query
letter.

THE CROSSROADS PUBLISHING COMPANY
370 Lexington Avenue
New York, New York 10017
(212) 532-3650

Michael Leach, Executive Vice President

Crossroads publishes scholarly books for seminarians, teachers,
and clergy, as well as for laypersons. Topics include theology,
history, spirituality, and world religions. Bible study materials
are also included in their list. Writers should send a query letter
and an initial outline.

CROSSWAY BOOKS (see GOOD NEWS PUBLISHERS)

DOUBLEDAY & COMPANY
Religion Publishing Group
245 Park Avenue
New York, New York 10167
(212) 953-4561

Robert T. Heller, Executive Editor

Doubleday & Company publishes material for scholarly biblical
commentaries as well as inspirational books relating to Jewish,
Catholic, and Evangelical groups. They wish to see a query,
chapter index, topic summary, and sample chapters.

WILLIAM B. EERDMANS PUBLISHING COMPANY
255 Jefferson Avenue, S.E.
Grand Rapids, Michigan 49503
(616) 459-4591

Jon Pott, Editor-in-Chief

Eerdmans publishes a wide range of religious literature for clergy and laity. Works they develop include theology, biblical studies, literature and the arts, some devotionals, and works on the social sciences. Send a query letter and two sample chapters.

FAIRWAY PRESS
Drawer L
Lima, Ohio 45802
(419) 227-1818

Greg Mikesell, Publisher

Fairway is associated with **C.S.S. PUBLISHERS,** and is the arm of the operation which publishes books on a cooperative basis, meaning that the author puts up some of the publishing cost.

FORTRESS PRESS
2900 Queen Lane
Philadelphia, Pennsylvania 19129
(215) 848-6800

Norman Hjelm, Director and Senior Editor

Fortress is the scholarly book publishing ministry of the Lutheran Church of America. They have a rather heavy emphasis on books for the academic market, including theology and biblical texts, church history studies, books for counselors and professors, some devotional materials, and studies in preaching and worship. It is best to send a query letter, abstract, and a couple of sample chapters.

GOOD NEWS PUBLISHERS/CROSSWAY BOOKS
9825 West Roosevelt Road
Westchester, Illinois 60153
(312) 345-7474

Jan P. Dennis, Editor-in-Chief

This publisher produces books of inspiration, contemporary problems handled in a biblical perspective, books of a conservative political nature which integrate Christianity, and some devotionals. They have a line of mainstream fiction for both youth and adults, and fantasy and science fiction for young adults. They will accept a query letter or the complete manuscript.

GOSPEL LIGHT PUBLICATIONS (see **REGAL BOOKS**)

GROUP BOOKS
P.O. Box 481
Loveland, Colorado 80539
(303) 669-3836

Lee Sparks, Editor

The emphasis for this house is on youth ministry. The books are geared to those who work with junior through senior high, mostly in a church setting. They are seeking how-to, devotionals, Bible studies, and reference. Query letters only.

HARPER & ROW PUBLISHERS
1700 Montgomery Street
San Francisco, California 94111
(415) 989-9000

John Loudon, Editorial Manager
Roy M. Carlisle, Editor
Becky Laird, Editor

Harper & Row is interested in serious theology and biblical studies, translations, religion and philosophy of religion, liturgy and preaching, and sociological and psychological studies. They also publish more popular materials for the general lay audience, and books on spirituality. They want to see an annotated outline, one or two sample chapters, and a curriculum vitae.

HARRISON HOUSE
P.O. Box 35035
Tulsa, Oklahoma 74153
(918) 582-2126

Sharon Seward, Production

This publisher wants Christian teaching books, and emphasizes the publishing of sermons. Send a query letter for first approach.

HARVARD UNIVERSITY PRESS
79 Garden Street
Cambridge, Massachusetts 02138
(617) 495-2600

Joan Mark, Editor

Harvard Press publishes several scholarly religious studies each year related to history, biblical studies, and other serious works. Authors must send a query letter indicating subject, treatment, length, plus a table of contents.

HARVEST HOUSE PUBLISHERS
1075 Arrowsmith
Eugene, Oregon 97402
(503) 343-0123

Eileen Mason, Editor

Harvest House does several adult and youth "how-to" books, as well as other more popular treatments of Christianity. All topics must be examined from a biblical standpoint with an emphasis on contemporary application. They wish to see an outline, project synopsis, and the first three chapters.

HENDRICKSON PUBLISHERS
One Scouting Way
Box 3473
Peabody, Massachusetts 01960-473
(617) 535-6437

Stephen J. Hendrickson, President

This house publishes books of a more academic perspective in the areas of Bible study, theology, philosophy, homiletics, and original language study (the biblical languages). Their current goal is to develop a more pentecostal line of materials. Send manuscripts.

HERALD PRESS
616 Walnut Avenue
Scottdale, Pennsylvania 15683
(412) 887-8500

Paul M. Schrock, General Book Editor

Herald, a subsidiary of **Mennonite Publishing House, Inc.**, does books for the general Christian public on themes that are important to Mennonites—discipleship, marriage and family, peace and the ethic of love, etc. They do juvenile, self-help, Bible study, personal experience, how-to, devotional and family living. Query with synopsis and SASE.

HERE'S LIFE PUBLISHERS
795 South Allen Street
P.O. Box 1576
San Bernardino, California 92402
(714) 886-7981

Leslie H. Stobbe, Editorial Director
Jean Bryant, Associate Editor

Here's Life is the book publishing affiliation of Campus Crusade for Christ, International. They publish books which speak to the spiritual needs of contemporary people, especially students, but are widening their list to the more general trade. Some of their titles include modern apologetics, adult Bible references, and how-to. They want books to move people to ministry and equip them with the tools for ministry. Send a letter requesting submission information.

HUNTINGTON HOUSE
1200 North Market Street
Shreveport, Louisiana 71107
(318) 221-2767

Bill Keith, Editor

This is a new publisher which specializes in the more popular and controversial religious books. They are looking for books of contemporary concerns, biographies, books on globalism and the "New Age" movement. Send query letters.

IMPACT BOOKS
365 Great Circle Road
Nashville, Tennessee 37228
(615) 327-2836

Sue Gay, Editor

The Impact line is now owned by **ZONDERVAN PUBLISHING**. They publish books of Bible studies, basic Christian beliefs, inspiration, humor and biography. Send manuscript proposal and author biography.

INSTITUTE OF SOCIAL SCIENCES AND ARTS, INC.
811 Magnolia Extention No. 45
Johnson City, Tennessee 37601
(615) 928-4003

Jonathan Donehoo, Executive Director

The Institute is a publisher which handles all kinds of books, religion being only one of their fields. The religious material published here is of a scholarly or academic nature. The board of editors actively seek a broad range of materials from authors working on projects of an intellectual nature. Since the subject matter of most of their books is very specialized, they do require a minimum order from the authors. Send vitae, brief outline or table of contents, and synopsis of chapters.

INTERVARSITY PRESS
Box 1400
Downers Grove, Illinois 60515
(312) 964-5700

James W. Sire, Editor

This press, affiliated with InterVarsity Fellowship, publishes books which will interest persons in academic circles, including clergy, laypeople, youth and adults of many denominations. Bible studies, apologetics, and books which explore contemporary issues from an evangelical standpoint are included in their list. Send a query letter, book synopsis, and sample chapter.

JONATHAN DAVID PUBLISHERS, INC.
68-22 Eliot Avenue
Middle Village, New York 11379
(212) 456-8611

D. Kay, Editor

This publisher is interested in devotional and issue-oriented Christian materials, as well as more general, secular books. They wish to see a query letter and project outline.

JUDSON PRESS
P.O. Box 851
Valley Forge, Pennslyvania 19482-0851
(215) 768-2121

Phyllis Frantz, Manuscript Editor

Judson is the publishing arm of the American Baptist Churches in the U.S.A. They publish books on social issues, worship aids, Bible studies, and resources for church leaders. Send a query letter, outline, and a single sample chapter.

JOHN KNOX PRESS
341 Ponce de Leon, N.E.
Atlanta, Georgia 30308
(404) 873-1531

Walt Sutton, Editor

John Knox is one of the official publishing agencies of the Presbyterian Church (U.S.A.). Most of their books are aimed at adult audiences and include scholars, students, clergy and laypeople. They are interested in books on Bible studies, theology, ethical issues, pastoral care, psychology of religion and worship. They request a query letter with sample chapters be sent for the first contact.

KREGEL PUBLICATIONS
733 Wealthy Street, S.E.
P.O. Box 2607
Grand Rapids, Michigan 49501
(616) 451-4775

Robert L. Kregel, President

Most of Kregel's list consists of reprints of Christian classics and religious commentaries. However, they do occasionally publish original projects for the general trade. Since they do not actively solicit many works, nor are they in the active market for solicitations, send a query letter first.

LIGUORI PUBLICATIONS
One Liguori Drive
Liguori, Missouri 63057
(314) 464-2500

Christopher Farrell, Editor-in-Chief

This publisher is operated by a Catholic religious order, the Redemptorists. They publish problem-oriented, self-help and devotional books. Curriculum and study guides are also published. All materials must be from a Catholic-Christian perspective. Query or submit outline/synopsis plus a sample chapter.

LION PUBLISHING COMPANY
10885 Textile
Belleville, Michigan 48111
(313) 483-8462

Tony Wales, Vice President

Lion is a British publisher which has now established an American office. They are looking for colorful books for juveniles and adults of all types - devotionals, self-help, fiction. Send full manuscript with cover letter.

LOIZEAUX BROTHERS, INC.
1238 Corlies Avenue
P.O. Box 277
Neptune, New Jersey 07753
(201) 774-8144

Peter Bartlett, Executive Vice President
Marie Loizeaux, Editor

Loizeaux publishes biblical commentaries and other books of serious Christian thought from a conservative, evangelical world view. Send query.

MACMILLAN PUBLISHING COMPANY, INC.
866 Third Avenue
New York, New York 10022
(212) 702-3285

Alexia Dor, Editor for Religious Books

Religious books at Macmillan are published out of the General Books Division, and include inspirational materials, Bible reference books, and books generally aimed at the religious trade. They do not do specific denominational or confessional titles. Query letter only.

MEADOWBROOK PRESS, INC.
18318 Minnetonka Blvd.
Deephaven, Minnesota 55391
(612) 473-5400

Kathe Grooms, Editorial Director

This general press publishes in the areas of child care and travel, and does some non-book projects, such as calendars. Send the manuscript along with a cover letter.

MENNONITE PUBLISHING HOUSE, INC.
(see **HERALD PRESS**)

MERCER UNIVERSITY PRESS
Mercer University
Macon, Georgia 31207
(912) 744-2880

Edd Rowell, Jr., Editor-in-Chief

Mercer University Press is especially interested in scholarly books in the fields of religion, including history, Bible studies and ethics. Submit outline/synopsis and sample chapters.

MOODY PRESS
2101 West Howard Street
Chicago, Illinois 60645
(312) 973-7800

Jerry B. Jenkins, Director
Jill Wilson, Adult Trade Editor

Moody Press is the publishing division for Moody Bible Institute. It publishes books of conservative evangelical concerns, including Bible commentaries, texts for colleges and seminaries, and general books on evangelism and worship aids. Their goal is to serve the Christian market with books that teach, encourage, strengthen, correct, comfort, inspire and edify. Query with outline and sample chapters.

MOREHOUSE-BARLOW CO.,INC.
78 Danbury Road
Wilton, Connecticut 06897
(203) 762-0721

Theodore A. McConnell, Editorial Director

This firm specializes in Anglican religious publishing, including titles representative of theology, religion, ethics, religious education, liturgics, primary and secondary texts. Submit full manuscript with SASE.

WILLIAM MORROW & COMPANY, INC., PUBLISHERS
105 Madison Avenue
New York, New York 10016
(212) 889-3050

Query c/o the Editorial Department

Morrow doesn't publish many religious books, and has no religious books division. But a query letter on books of a more general religious nature will be entertained. The general trade division publishes religion, along with fiction, poetry, arts, history and how-to books. Manuscripts and proposals should be submitted through a literary agent.

MOTT MEDIA, INC., PUBLISHERS
1000 East Huron Street
Milford, Michigan 48042
(313) 685-8773

Leonard George Goss, Senior Editor

Mott Media publishes books for the Christian trade and for Christian schools. (The company also owns and operates the **Evangelical Book Club,** one of the premier religious book clubs in the country.) Trade projects should be orthodox in Christian doctrine, with sound exegesis and logical and practical application for all readers. Classroom and supplementary materials should be geared to the Christian school movement.

Prospective authors should send a brief description of the contents of their writing project, an assessment of the basic readership, and a short explanation of why the manuscript differs from other books on the subject.

MULTNOMAH PRESS
10209 S.E. Division Street
Portland, Oregon 97266
(503) 257-0526

John Van Diest, Vice President of Literature Ministries
John Sloan, Editor

This press is the publishing ministry of the Multnomah School of the Bible. It wishes to provide literature that is contemporary while remaining faithful to the Scriptures. It publishes books of biblical studies, critical social concerns, Christian growth, family enrichment, and religious texts. Query letter only.

NAVPRESS
3820 North 30th Street
P.O. Box 6000
Colorado Springs, Colorado 80934
(303) 598-1212

Donald Simpson, Managing Editor

NavPress develops materials on discipleship and Bible study. Send a query letter, an outline, and sample chapters.

NAZARENE PUBLISHING HOUSE
2923 Troost Avenue
P.O. Box 527
Kansas City, Missouri 64109
(816) 931-1900

M.A. Lunn, Coordinator of Book Publications

The Nazarene Publishing House operates under the trade logo of **Beacon Hill Press of Kansas City**, and is the publishing arm of the Church of the Nazarene. They publish a wide range of material from juvenile to college texts. The scope includes inspirational, devotional, Bible study and beliefs. Interested also in social action themes. They want writers to use the query approach, but include a couple of sample chapters.

THOMAS NELSON PUBLISHERS, INC.
P.O. Box 141000
Nelson Place at Elm Hill Pike
Nashville, Tennessee 37214-1000
(615) 889-9000

Lawrence M. Stone, Vice President Editorial
Peter Gillquist, Religious Book Editor
Ronald E. Pitkin, Academic and Reference Books Editor

Thomas Nelson, one of the oldest publishing firms in the country, publishes books for adult readers, and includes in its list of books those of historic Christian belief, and the validity of Christian experience. They want orthodoxy, honesty, quality and validity. Query letter and outline only.

OMEGA PUBLICATIONS
P.O. Box 4130
Medford, Oregon 97510
(503) 826-9279

Jim Andrews, President

Omega publishes books with a heavy emphasis on popular end-time themes, and also does some Bible study and family-related material. Send manuscripts.

ORBIS BOOKS
Maryknoll, New York 10545
(914) 941-7590

John Eagleson, Editor

Orbis does religious studies and theology from and on Asia, Africa, and Latin America. Their emphasis is on the First

World response to the Third World challenge relating to religious justice and peace themes. Send a query letter, outline, and sample chapters.

OXFORD UNIVERSITY PRESS
200 Madison Avenue
New York, New York 10016
(212) 679-7300

Cynthia Read, Editor

Oxford's emphasis now is on scholarly textbooks, historical studies (American religion), Biblical studies and theological works. They wish to see a query letter, outline and sample chapters.

PAULIST PRESS
545 Island Road
Ramsey, New Jersey 07446
(201) 825-7300

Kevin A. Lynch, Editor

Paulist is a Catholic publisher, but its titles are not limited to Catholic interests alone. They aim at a broad ecumenical market and publish a variety of religious material ranging from serious theology/academic works to some popular spirituality/inspirational. They also do church history, biblical studies and exegesis. Send query, outline, sample chapter.

PELICAN PUBLISHING COMPANY
1101 Monroe Street
Gretna, Louisiana 70053
(504) 368-1175

Frumie Selchen, Editor

Pelican has a Baptist orientation but publishes books for a variety of lay readers as well as the clergy. Bible studies and especially self-help and motivational books are among their releases. Submit outline/synopsis and sample chapters.

PENTECOSTAL PUBLISHING HOUSE
8855 Dunn Road
Hazelwood, Missouri 63042
(314) 837-7300

J.O. Wallace, General Manager

Also publishing under the name **World Aflame Press**, this house looks for manuscripts covering Protestant religion, Bible study, crafts and self-help. Send query.

PILGRIM PRESS
132 West 31st Street
New York, New York 10001
(212) 594-8555

Marion M. Meyer, Senior Editor

Pilgrim publishes books on energy, social issues, church growth, education and women's issues, among other categories. They are the publishing arm of the United Church Board of Home Missions (United Church of Christ). Send query letter only.

PINE MOUNTAIN PRESS, INC.
P.O. Box 19746
West Allis, Wisconsin 53219
(414) 778-1120

Robert W. Pradt, Publisher

This is a general publisher for whom religion is a relatively new field. They are interested in inspirational material and some biblical studies. They wish to see a query letter first.

PRENTICE-HALL, INC.
Englewood Cliffs, New Jersey 07632
(201) 592-2000

Raymond T. O'Connell, Editor

Prentice-Hall publishes religious books primarily for clergy and scholarly audiences, but they are also interested in inspirational guides for women, Bible study materials, and religious books generally applicable to living in today's world. Their texts for the academic setting include studies in history, biblical studies, theology and some reference works. Query letters only.

PRESBYTERIAN AND REFORMED PUBLISHING COMPANY
Box 817
Phillipsburg, New Jersey 08865
(201) 454-0505

Thom Notaro, Editor

Presbyterian and Reformed is not owned by any denomination, but is affiliated by worldview with those groups which follow the Westminster Confession of Faith. Therefore, all their books are consistent with that Confession, in both the shorter and larger catechisms. They are looking for books on theology, eschatology, the biblical perspective on social issues, church management, and pastoral textbooks. They have also published under the **Craig Press** imprint. Send manuscript proposal and SASE.

REGAL BOOKS
2300 Knoll Drive
Ventura, California 93006
(805) 644-9721

Donald E. Pugh, Senior Editor

Regal Books, a division of **Gospel Light**, aims its list primarily at lay audiences with the goal being to help them grow in Christian faith and knowledge. Included in their publishing list are books dealing with missions, Bible studies, self-help, Christian living and church growth books. Query or submit outline/synopsis and sample chapters.

FLEMING H. REVELL COMPANY
184 Central Avenue
P.O. Box 150
Old Tappan, New Jersey 07675
(201) 768-8060

Norma Chimento, Managing Editor
Fritz Ridenour, Field Editor

Revell, now owned by **Zondervan**, is interested in books for adult laypersons. Most of their books appeal to the Protestant-evangelical tradition, and should demonstrate the message of Christian salvation. Books which show how Christ has changed or stregthened lives are especially welcomed. Their imprints also include **Power Books** and **Spire**. Send a query letter.

ROPER PRESS
915 Dragon Street
Dallas, Texas 75207
(214) 742-6696

Billy O. Hoskins, President

This is primarily a curriculum house which does curricula for various grades of Sunday School. Send a query letter.

SCHOCKEN BOOKS, INC.
200 Madison Avenue
New York, New York 10016
(212) 685-6500

Bonny Fetterman, Religious Editor

Most of Schocken's books cover the Judaic market, both ancient and modern studies. They have also done books on the Gospels, however. Send query letter only.

SCRIPTURE PRESS (see **VICTOR BOOKS**)

SERENDIPITY, INC.
2550 West Main Street
P.O. Box 1012
Littleton, Colorado 80160
(303) 798-1313

Lyman Coleman, President

This company is looking for Bible study group curriculum for both youth and adults. Query only.

SERVANT PUBLICATIONS
840 Airport Blvd.
P.O. Box 8617
Ann Arbor, Michigan 48107
(313) 761-8505

Ann Spangler, Associate Editor

Servant publishes books on practical Christian teaching including biblical studies, meditations, works on prayer, the Church today, and the Charismatic movement. Send query letter and outline.

HAROLD SHAW PUBLISHERS
388 Gundersen Drive
P.O. Box 567
Wheaton, Illinois 60189
(312) 665-6700

Megs Singer, Managing Editor

This publisher is interested in books which help people live the Christian faith in a work-a-day world. Some devotional reading is produced, and Bible studies, along with reference works. Basically, they want books of general interest to Christians. Send synopsis and sample chapters.

STANDARD PUBLISHING COMPANY
8121 Hamilton Avenue
Cincinnati, Ohio 45231
(513) 931-4050

Marge Miller, Director, New Product Development

Standard issues books of fiction and nonfiction for a wide audience from children to senior citizens. Their books include church growth, leadership in the body of Christ, and deeper spiritual life. Clergy and laity of mainline Protestant denominations, Evangelical, and Roman Catholic churches are represented in Standard's list of authors. Query letter only.

SWEET PUBLISHING COMPANY
7434 Tower
Ft. Worth, Texas 76118
(817) 595-2667

Bill New, President

Sweet's market is very specific: Bible school curriculum. Ninety-five percent of their material is produced for the Church of Christ. Query.

TRINITY HOUSE
5311 Montfort Lane
P. O. Box 104
Crestwood, Kentucky 40014
(502) 241-1492

Woody McGraw, President

This publisher is looking for nonfiction "how-to" books; practical, easy to understand materials on marriage, counseling, finances, etc. They are also open to expanding their list beyond the "how-to." Send full manuscripts and cover letter.

TYNDALE HOUSE PUBLISHERS
336 Gundersen Drive
Wheaton, Illinois 60187
(312) 668-8300

Wendell Hawley, Editor-in-Chief
Virginia Muir, Senior Editor for Special Projects

Tyndale publishes general nonfiction religious devotional/
inspirational books, and some reference material. They publish
no material for children under 12 years of age. Query letter
with a couple of completed chapters.

UNIVERSITY PRESS OF AMERICA
4720 Boston Way
Lanham, Maryland 20706
(301) 459-3366

Helen Hudson, Editorial Assistant

This publisher issues religious books for non-denominational,
academic classroom use. Among the interests of this publisher
are books in biblical studies, philosophy of religion, history,
comparative religions, theology and language studies. They will
accept a query letter or synopsis, but they prefer getting a copy
of the entire manuscript.

THE UPPER ROOM
1908 Grand Avenue
Nashville, Tennessee 37202
(615) 327-2700

Charla H. Honea, Editorial Assistant

The Upper Room is the devotional publishing arm of the
United Methodist Church. Their publishing emphasis is on
inspirational material for Christians. They prefer that authors
approach them through the query letter.

VICTOR BOOKS
1825 College Avenue
Wheaton, Illinois 60187
(312) 668-6000

James R. Adair, Executive Editor
Carole S. Streeter, Senior Acquisitions Editor

Victor publishes biblically-based books with a contemporary message aimed at the man or woman in the local church. The audience is primarily adults and youth of mainline Protestant denominations. Victor is the book publishing division of the evangelical curriculum publisher, **Scripture Press.** They wish to see a query letter, curriculum vitae, outline, project summary and sample chapter.

VISION HOUSE PUBLISHERS, INC.
2691 Richter Avenue, Suite 117
Irvine, California 92714
(714) 863-9440

John M. Montgomery, President

Vision House is now a division of **Gospel Light Publications.** They do books for the lay audience, primarily in the area of psychological helps and testimony books. They want materials which will tie into their tape and video program. Send a query letter.

WESTMINSTER PRESS
925 Chestnut Street
Philadelphia, Pennsylvania 19107
(215) 928-2725

Keith Crim, Editorial Director

Westminster is the publishing arm of the Presbyterian Church, U.S.A. Their publishing program includes books of current social and religious interest, including Christianity in Third World countries. Present-day ethical issues for scholars, church professionals, and general laypersons are well received in their market. They have a wide latitude on the interpretation of religious truth. Query letter with synopsis is required.

WHITAKER HOUSE
Pittsburg and Colfax Streets
Springdale, Pennsylvania 15144
(412) 274-4440

Donna Arthur, Administrative Editor

This publisher produces books which reflect various aspects of life in Christ, and books on family life. Charismatic literature is an area of main interest for Whitaker House. Query letter only.

WINSTON PRESS
430 Oak Grove
Minneapolis, Minnesota 55403
(612) 871-7000

Wayne Paulson, Trade Editor

Winston is a unit of CBS Educational and Professional Publishing which produces books in religion, self-help and human behavior and development. They also publish preschool, elementary and secondary school curriculum. This house is trying to bridge the gap between the Catholic and Evangelical markets. Send query, samples and SASE.

WORD BOOKS, PUBLISHER
4800 West Waco Drive
Waco, Texas 76710
(817) 772-7650

Al Bryant, Managing Editor

Word publishes materials which have to do with personal growth in Christ, Bible studies, theology, family life, and Christian lifestyles. The audience is predominately adults of mainline Protestant evangelical groups. A query letter should be sent, along with two or three sample chapters.

WORLD AFLAME PRESS (see **PENTECOSTAL PUBLISHING HOUSE**)

YALE UNIVERSITY PRESS
92A Yale Station
New Haven, Connecticut 06520
(203) 432-4969

Charles Grench, Editor

The religious books published by Yale are academic books for scholars and academic communities, but some books are done for the general audience. Their mix includes archaeology, biblical exposition and history of early Christianity. Send a query letter plus a prospectus and a curriculum vitae.

ZONDERVAN PUBLISHING HOUSE
1415 Lake Drive, S.E.
Grand Rapids, Michigan 49506
(616) 459-6900

James E. Ruark, Senior Editor
Kin Millen, Acquisitions Editor

The Zondervan firm publishes books that take a fresh approach to issues and problems for the evangelical Protestant audience. They introduce books of Bible studies, family life (they are looking for new, but biblical, angles on family life), language aids, theology, professional reference, evangelism, church growth and personal faith. Some fiction is also published, but is not as much of a special interest to Zondervan as the foregoing. They wish to see a table of contents and a summary of each chapter of your writing project.

A NOTE: Market conditions are constantly changing. To stay current, we recommend the market guide service available from the Christian Writers Institute. The service supplies you with approximately 300 continually updated and current markets. All entries are kept up to date on a quarterly basis. To subscribe, write to: Market Guide, Christian Writers Institute, 396 East St. Charles Road, Wheaton, Illinois, 60188.

Chapter 9

SELECTIVE BIBLIOGRAPHY:
Some of the Better Books
on Writing and Publishing

SELECTIVE BIBLIOGRAPHY: Some of the Better Books on Writing and Publishing

The following books are especially helpful and interesting. This is a subjective opinion, of course, but all opinions are subjective. Some of these titles are out of print, so you will have to check your local library. But most are available, and may either be consulted in a good library or ordered from most any bookstore. If you are interested in buying some of the out of print ones, try a place known as The Scribbling Bookmonger, Route 28A, Box 40, West Shokan, New York 12494. This shop specializes in used books on writing. They will be happy to add your name to their mailing list. Be sure to peruse the October, 1981 issue of *Writer's Digest* for a wide sampling of reference books and journals. It is quite useful.

The Art and Science of Book Publishing, by Herbert S. Bailey, Jr. (New York: Harper & Row Publishers, 1970; Austin, Texas: University of Texas Press, 1982). A rigorous introduction to the editorial, production and especially business aspects of publishing.

The Associated Press Guide to Good Writing, by Rene J. Cappon (Reading, Ma.: Addison-Wesley Publishing Company, 1982). The how-to on reports, stories, articles and presentations from the world's largest newsgathering organization.

The Associated Press Stylebook and Libel Manual, edited by
C. W. French, E. A. Powell and H. Angione (Reading, Ma.:
Addison-Wesley Publishing Company, 1982). Authoritative
word on the rules of grammar, punctuation and the general
meaning and usage of over 3,000 terms. Extensive
bibliography full of research sources.

An Author's Primer to Word Processing, Association of
American Publishers (New York: AAP, 1983). If you are
tempted to prepare your manuscript electronically, but do
not know where to begin what with the many systems on
the market, this valuable overview is for you. Here is a
painless way to find out what the machines can do.

Author Law & Strategies, by Brad Bunnin and Peter Beren
(Berkeley, Ca.: Nolo Press, 1983). An outstanding legal
guide for the working writer. All areas are covered.

The Art of Persuasion, by Steward LaCasce and Terry Belanger
(New York: Charles Scribner's Sons, 1972). The authors
show speakers and writers how to utilize the psychological
techniques of persuasion.

Becoming a Writer, by Dorothea Brande (Los Angeles: J.P.
Tarcher, Inc., 1934, reissued 1981). Here is an excellent look
at the process of becoming a writer. One becomes a writer
through work, but as Brande points out, the journey is worth
the effort. The sections on creativity are especially good.

The Beginning Writer's Answer Book, edited by Kirk Polking,
Jean Chimsky and Rose Adkins (Cincinnati, Ohio: Writer's
Digest Books, 1978 revised edition). Written in a question
and answer format, this book contains various pointers and
answers questions for beginning writers.

The Blockbuster Complex, by Thomas Whiteside (Middletown,
Ct.: Wesleyan University Press, 1981). The "big deals" side
of publishing is here explored. Nearly all of the material
appeared originally in *The New Yorker*.

Book Publishing: What It Is, What It Does, by John P.
Dessauer (New York: R.R. Bowker, 2nd Edition, 1981). The
author is one of the publishing industry's best students.

Book Reviewing, edited by Sylvia E. Kammerman (Boston, Ma.: The Writer, Inc., 1978). Twenty book editors, critics and reviewers offer this comprehensive guide to writing proper book reviews for newspapers, magazines, radio and television. From short descriptions to the critical essay, everything about reviewing is covered here.

Books: The Culture and Commerce of Publishing, by Lewis Coser, Charles Kadushin and Walter Powell (New York: Basic Books, 1982). The entire spectrum of book publishing is studied by three sociologists.

Breaking Into Print, by Philip J. Gearing and Evelyn V. Brunson (Englewood Cliffs, New Jersey: Prentice-Hall, 1977). This is an excellent "how-to" guide for beginning writers of books.

The Business of Being a Writer, by Stephen Goldin and Kathleen Sky (New York: Harper & Row Publishers, 1982). The authors dish up a "meat-and-potatoes" book, basic and essential. As the title indicates, this work is about the business side of writing, things such as copyrighting, contracts, agents, record keeping, taxes and so on.

Celebrating Children's Books, edited by Betsy Hearne and Marilyn Kaye (New York: Lathrop, Lee & Shepard Books, 1981). Good criticism of children's literature, for all who care about the books that children read. For the people who create, produce and use them.

The Chicago Manual of Style, 13th Edition, prepared by the Editorial Staff of the University of Chicago Press (Chicago: University of Chicago Press, 1982). Standard reference tool for all authors, editors, copywriters and proofreaders. The 13th Edition is the first revision since 1969. Get this justly famous volume.

The Christian Writer's Handbook, by Margaret J. Anderson (San Francisco, Ca.: Harper & Row Publishers, 2nd Edition, 1983). Beneficial for all who write articles in general, and for the Christian markets in particular. From style to author's rights.

Communication Theory for Christian Witness, by Charles H. Kraft (Nashville, Tn.: Abingdon Press, 1983). Introduces the reader to modern communication theory through the skillful use of examples drawn from modern living and the Bible. Helps in overcoming barriers to communication and in moving toward a more effective Christian witness.

The Complete Guide to Writing Nonfiction, edited by Glen Evans for the American Society of Journalists and Authors, (Cincinnati, Ohio: Writer's Digest Books, 1983). 108 professional writers give a total guide to today's world of nonfiction, including a chapter on writing religion. Massive and worthwhile.

Confessions of a Moonlight Writer, by James H. Cox (Brentwood, Tn.: J.M. Productions, 1981). If your interest is in writing for the church market, this book is for you. It is a practical road map for novices.

The Craft of Non-Fiction, by William C. Knott (Reston, Va.: Reston Publishing Company, 1974). This little book is an introduction to the craft of writing nonfiction material.

The Creative Writer, edited by Aron Mathieu (Cincinnati, Ohio: Writer's Digest Books, 1961). This book is a collection of articles from masters of writing on everything from plotting a novel to writing for the theater. Other sections treat the topics of working with editors, writing articles, and practical issues.

Directory of Historical Societies and Agencies in the United States and Canada, edited by Tracey Lenton Craig (Nashville, Tn.: American Association for State and Local History, 12th Edition, 1982). This directory lists over 4,000 historical societies, archives, record centers and the like. Marvelous for historical research.

The Elements of Editing: A Modern Guide for Editors and Journalists, by Arthur Plotnik (New York: Macmillan Publishing Company, 1982). A fun-to-read, informal guide in the tradition of Struck and White's *The Elements of Style*, and also an inside look at editing and editorial advice. Writers and editors should have this.

The Elements of Style, 3rd Edition, by William Strunk, Jr., and E.B. White (New York: Macmillan Publishing Company, 1979). The most acclaimed and indispensable small style manual. Always have it on hand.

Finding Facts, by William L. Rivers (Englewood Cliffs, New Jersey: Prentice-Hall, 1975). Rivers shows you how to excavate useful information from various sources. This is a valuable resource book.

Finding Facts Fast, by Alden Todd (Berkeley, Ca.: Ten Speed Press, 1979). This is one of the finest guides to fact-gathering techniques in a "how to do it" format.

Freelance Writing: Advice From the Pros, by Curtis W. Casewit (New York: Collier Books, 1974). Many successful writers, through the author, give advice on the marketing of all types of writing. Covers research aids, book and article writing, specialty writing, interview techniques, finances, royalties and subsidiary rights, and much more.

Getting Published, by David St. John Thomas and Hubert Bermont (New York: Harper & Row Publishers, 1973). This book is a frank and realistic view of what getting published takes. It is not discouraging but it is honest in pointing out that not every writer will get published.

Getting Your Foot in the Editorial Door, by Thomas A. Noton (Lakeland, Fl.: TCW Marketing Group, 1983). Get beyond the amateur appearance and production job on this book, and you will find often valuable step-by-step advice on understanding and approaching editors and publishers. The book takes much of the mythology out of the publishing field for new writers.

Handbook For Christian Writers, compiled by the Christian Writers Institute (Carol Stream, Ill.: Creation House, 3rd Edition, 1973). This book is a collection of tips, ideas and markets for the beginning writer of Christian literature.

How I Write, by Robert J. Hastings (Nashville, Tn.: Broadman Press, 1973). This is an amusing and inspiring "how to" guide for beginners. It is full of illustrations and ideas.

How To Be An Author, by Denys Val Baker (London: Harvill Press, 1952). Baker offers this slightly tongue-in-cheek guide which tells you exactly how *not* to do it.

How To Get Happily Published, by Judith Appelbaum and Nancy Evans (New York: Harper & Row Publishers, 1978). The title describes exactly what the authors attempt in this volume. The style is lively and interesting, and the information is invaluable.

How To Get Started in Writing, by Peggy Teeters (Cincinnati, Ohio: Writer's Digest Books, 1982). Step by step through the writing and publishing process, starting with small projects to help you build confidence as a writer.

How to Make Money Writing Little Articles, Anecdotes, Hints, Recipes, Light Verse, and Other Fillers, by Connie Emerson (Cincinnati, Ohio: Writer's Digest Books, 1983). Shows how various short articles can be a profitable source of income. There is good instruction covering both writing and marketing angles.

How To Read Slowly: A Christian Guide to Reading with the Mind, by James W. Sire (Downers Grove, Ill.: Inter-Varsity Press, 1979). Through practical chapters on reading fiction, nonfiction, poetry and other material, readers are offered counsel on understanding not only what writers say but what lies behind what they say. This title has been reprinted by Multnomah Press as **The Joy of Writing: A Guide to Becoming a Better Reader.**

How To Stop A Sentence (and Other Methods of Managing Words), by Nora Gallagher (Reading, Ma.: Addison-Wesley Publishing Company, 1982). A fun and foundational guide to good punctuation, useful for the novice as brush-up.

How To Use the Federal FOI Act (Washington: FOI Service Center, 1125 15th Street, N.W., 20005, @50¢). Have you ever wondered how to take advantage of the Freedom of Information Act? This book will tell you how.

How To Write Non-Fiction That Sells, by F.A. Rockwell (Chicago: Henry Regnery Company, 1975). The title is the gist.

How You Can Make $20,000 A Year Writing, by Nancy Edmonds Hanson (Cincinnati, Ohio: Writer's Digest Books,1980). Hanson offers a variety of ways to make income at writing.

If I Can Write, You Can Write, by Charlie Shedd (Cincinnati, Ohio: Writer's Digest Books, 1984). Shedd takes would-be writers over the hurdles of discouragement to the conviction that they, too, can be writers. He paints no rosy pictures, but gives a unique blend of instruction and inspiration.

In Cold Type: Overcoming the Book Crisis, by Leonard Shatzkin (Boston, Ma.: Houghton Mifflin Company, 1982). A controversial examination of the practices and problems of an industry in crisis. Advocates the expanded use of computers for analysis and operational control to salvage publishing's appalling inefficiency.

In The Minister's Workshop, by Halford E. Luccock (Nashville, Tn.: Abingdon Press, 1944; Reprinted by Baker Book House). This is actually a guide to preaching, but Luccock has several helpful chapters on writing. His style is well worth studying.

Inside Publishing, by Bill Adler (New York: Bobbs-Merrill, 1982). A chatty, "insiders" look at what publishing is all about. Adler is one of the big-name New York agents.

An Introduction to Christian Writing, by Ethel Herr (Wheaton, Ill.: Tyndale House Publishers, 1983). A helpful do-it-yourself introductory writing text for those asking the question,"Do I want to be a writer?" Emphasizes writing as a ministry.

Literary Market Place (New York: R.R. Bowker Company, annual). This is a thorough listing of publishers, agents, printers, and markets. A hefty price, but the best resource you will find.

The Little Rhetoric and Handbook, by Edward P.J. Corbett (New York: John Wiley & Sons, Inc., 1977). From grammar, style, paragraphing, punctuation and mechanics, to the overall process of effective writing. A great, basic aid.

Max Perkins: Editor of Genius, by Scott Berg (New York: E.P. Dutton & Company, Inc., 1978). A moving biography of a truly great editor, full of interesting background on the book trade. Some of the literary careers Perkins nourished were Fitzgerald, Hemingway, Thomas Wolfe, Sherwood Anderson and Taylor Caldwell.

The Modern Researcher, by Jacques Barzun and Henry F. Graff (New York: Harcourt Brace Jovanovich, Inc., 3rd Edition, 1977). This book is a standard in the field of research. The authors offer a thorough guide to fact-gathering and interpretation. Read this one.

The New York Times Guide to Reference Material, by Mona McCormick (New York: Popular Library, 1982). McCormick offers a wealth of resource and reference material useful to any writer.

The Non-Fiction Book: How to Write and Sell It, by Paul R. Reynolds (New York: William Morrow & Company, 1970). Here is a broad discussion of how to research, organize, write and revise the original draft of a manuscript. Many good illustrations are used to explain the specific advice given in the first section. The second section describes how the author should approach publishers and agents.

Nonfiction: From Idea to Published Book, by Harry Edward Neal (New York: Wilfred Funk, Inc., 1964). Neal gives the beginner an idea of what he or she is up against in the writing business. An older book for this discussion, but still valuable.

On Writing Well, by William Zinsser (New York: Harper & Row Publishers, 2nd Edition, 1980). If you need to brush up on your writing skills, this book is perhaps the first one to turn to.

Opportunities in Book Publishing, by John Tebbel (Skokie, Ill.: National Textbook Company, 1980). The making and marketing of books requires the talents of a great many people—editors, copyeditors, graphic designers, typesetters, publicity and promotion people, production personnel, and salespersons. Many writers have found that book publishing offers a creative career in an interesting field. This vocational guidance manual sets the stage.

Opportunities in Free-Lance Writing, by Hazel Carter Maxon (Louisville, Kentucky: Data Courier, Inc., 1977). Do you have in mind earning a living as a free-lance writer? How do you find and maintain markets for your work? This is a compact guide to opportunities in full-time or part-time freelancing. Much of practical use for both the fiction and the factual writer, particularly the newcomer.

People, Books and Book People, by David W. McCullough (New York: Harmony Books, 1980). This is an anthology of interviews McCullough conducted with 90 authors. It is intimate and revealing about what it takes to be a writer.

Practical Guide for the Christian Writer, by David S. McCarthy (Valley Forge, Pa.: Judson Press, 1983). The author takes you through each step of the writing process from basic planning to hints for getting your manuscript accepted. A positive-attitude approach to writing as ministry.

The Religious Writers Marketplace, by William H. Gentz and Elaine W. Colvin (Philadelphia, Pa.: Running Press, 1980). This is a recent guide to markets and general information about the religious market. Over 1500 sources are listed here. Though already somewhat dated, it is well worth the price. A 1985 revised edition is available, however, late in 1984.

Sell Copy, by Webster Kuswa (Cincinnati, Ohio: Writer's Digest Books, 1979). Kuswa offers advice and strategies on writing material which will sell.

The Successful Writers & Editors Guidebook: Guide to Writing for the Growing Religious Market, edited by R.W. Walker, J. Franzen and H. Kidd (Carol Stream, Ill.: Creation House, 1977). 64 writing and publishing professionals offer a guide which is chock-full of writing and selling tips. Over 300 religious markets for books and articles.

Successful Writers and How They Work, by Larsten D. Farrar (New York: Hawthorne Books, 1959). Farrar pulls together advice and tips from established writers from many fields. Norman Vincent Peale, Sloan Wilson, Abigail Van Buren, and Jesse Stuart are some of the people cited here.

United States Government Organizational Manual (Washington: U.S. Government Printing Office, annual). Updated annually, this book gives background information on each of the government's various agencies. It has a list of names, addresses, and phone numbers of the press officers of those agencies.

Wanted: Writers for the Christian Market, by Mildred Schell (Valley Forge, Pa.: Judson Press, 1975). This book has two main sections: The first deals with the writer; the second deals with different kinds of writing. The bibliography, although dated, is still useful.

What Is An Editor?: Saxe Commins At Work, by Dorothy Commins (Chicago: University of Chicago Press, 1978). An unusually good survey of the publishing process by looking at one of the outstanding literary editors of Random House who influenced such personalities as Dreiser, Faulkner, O'Neill, Michener and many others.

What's Really Involved in Writing and Selling Your Book, by Robert Aldleman (Los Angeles: Nash Publishing Corporation, 1972). This is a step-by-step guide in coming up with an initial idea for a book all the way to seeing it in print. The style is question and answer, and the author knows what he is talking about.

Where to Go For What, by Mara Miller (Englewood Cliffs, New Jersey: Prentice-Hall, 1981). Miller offers guidance on basic research skills and techniques.

Write for the Religion Market, John A. Moore (Palm Springs, Ca.: ETC Publications, 1981). Moore tells how to write specifically for religious periodical and news markets. He demonstrates various ways to write a news story, a feature article, how to conduct an interview, and how to develop a personal style.

Write The Word, by William Folprecht (Milford, Michigan: Mott Media, Inc., Publishers, 1976). A guide for the author including information on marketing, writer's clubs and conferences, and agents. Offers advice about word awareness, vocabulary development, finding ideas, and submitting manuscripts.

Write On Target, by Sue Spencer (Waco, Texas: Word Books, Inc., 1976). Want to read a fun book on writing? This is it. Spencer spins a 120 page web of good writing about good writing.

Writers and Writing, by Robert Van Gelder (New York: Charles Scribner's Sons, 1946). This book is a compilation of interviews the author had with many of the best known writers of the first half of this century.

The Writer's Book, edited by Helen Hull (New York: Barnes & Noble, 1956). The Authors Guild presents this book as a helping hand to fledgling writers. Pearl Buck, Thomas Mann, James A. Michener and W.H. Auden are some of the 40 people who have contributed to this well-rounded book.

A Writer's Capital, by Louis Auchincloss (Boston, Ma.: Houghton Mifflin Company, 1974). This is the memoir of a well known author giving his origin and development as a writer. The title is from the saying, "It has been said that his childhood is a writer's entire capital."

The Writer's Craft, edited by John Hersey (New York: Alfred A. Knopf, 1974). A distinguished writer and teacher offers insights into what it means to live by and for the craft of writing. A galaxy of writing stars give an accounting of the work they do and how they do it.

Writer's Encyclopedia, edited by Kirk Polking (Cincinnati, Ohio: Writer's Digest Books, 1983). 1,200 alphabetical entries to explain writing terms. Offers information or tells you where to get it. Comprehensive reference for all who write.

A Writer's Guide to Book Publishing, by Richard Balkin (New York: Hawthorne/Dutton, 1981). Written by a literary agent, this book is a solid introduction to the various facets of book publishing, and includes sections on manuscript preparation, contracts, and so on. A lucid survey and a popular textbook in publishing courses.

The Writer's Handbook, edited by S.K. Burack (Boston, Ma.: The Writer, Inc., annual). A standard in the field, this annually revised handbook offers about two-thirds of its 700+ pages to articles on writing, and about one third to markets. You cannot go wrong in buying this one.

Writer's Market, edited by P.J. Schemenaur and John Brady (Cincinnati, Ohio: Writer's Digest Books, annual). Many writers regard this as *the* guide for all of the most used markets for all genre. It is updated annually.

Writer's Resource Guide, edited by Bernadine Clark (Cincinnati, Ohio: Writer's Digest Books, 1982). Are you looking for information on zoos, embassies, museums, libraries, government information agencies? If so, this guide is for you. Over 1,600 sources of research information.

Writer's Roundtable, edited by Helen Hull and Michael Drury (New York: Harper & Brothers, 1959). This is a potpourri of information on writing, writers and more technical matters.

The Writer's Survival Guide, by Jean Rosenbaum and Veryl Rausenbaum (Cincinnati, Ohio: Writer's Digest Books, 1982). This is one of the finest books on the more personal side of writing. The authors, one a psychiatrist and the other a psychoanalyst, deal with the author's personal and psychic life. Creativity, competitiveness, how rejections should be handled, developing a support system, and dealing with success are some of the topics covered in this excellent book.

Writing and Selling a Nonfiction Book, by Max Gunther (Boston, Ma.: The Writer, Inc., 1973). Step-by-step, practical guide to writing successfully for one of today's most receptive markets. Chapters include scope, technique and style in book writing.

Writing: Craft and Art, by William L. Rivers (Englewood Cliffs, New Jersey: Prentice-Hall, 1975). Rivers's book is a more generalized look at the craft of writing. Although an introduction, it is nevertheless helpful.

Writing for Publication, by Donald MacCampbell (New York: World Publishing Company, 1966). MacCampbell is a successful agent in New York. He gives an inside look at the world of book publishing.

Writing for the Joy of It: A Guide for Amateurs, by Leonard
L. Knott (Cincinnati, Ohio: Writer's Digest Books, 1983).
Knott says that writing for fun, not just for profit, is a
worthy goal. He helps you to develop and evaluate your pro-
gress as a writer through poetry, letters, journals and
autobiography.

Writing in America, by Erskin Caldwell (New York: Phaedra
Publishers, 1967). Written slightly tongue-in-cheek, this
book will tell you how to be a writer in America and live!

*Writing to Inspire: A Guide to Writing and Publishing for the
Expanding Religious Market*, edited by William Gentz (Cincinnati, Ohio: Writer's Digest Books, 1982). The subtitle
gives the story. From 30 leading inspirational writers comes
sometimes essential advice. Covers all types of religious
writing.

Writing to Sell, by Scott Meredith (New York: Harper & Row
Publishers, 2nd edition, 1974). Meredith is one of
publishing's most successful literary agents. His advice to
those interested in making their living in writing is directed
mostly to fiction writers, but there is much helpful material
for the nonfiction specialist as well. Good information on
marketing practices, working habits, manuscript preparation, etc.

Writing With Power, by Peter Elbow (New York: Oxford
University Press, 1981). This is a manual on the techniques
of writing. Even the most experienced writer could benefit
from this book.

You Can Tell The World, by Sherwood E. Wirt, with Ruth
McKinney (Minneapolis, Mn.: Augsburg Publishing House,
1975). This book is aimed especially at the Christian writer.
It is practical and inspirational, offering general guidelines
for writing and publishing.

EPILOGUE

EPILOGUE

Our purpose in writing this book has been to share with you some of our excitement about writing. We will have succeeded or failed depending on whether or not you have been helped by our attempts.

If you have any comments, suggestions, complaints or whatever about the book, please feel free to make them to us personally. You may write either or both of us in care of the publisher: Mott Media, Inc., 1000 East Huron Street, Milford, Michigan 48042. If you have something published as a result of reading this book, let us know and we will rejoice with you.

We will look forward to getting to know many of you personally as we attend various writing workshops and conferences where we speak. May God bless your efforts.

Don M. Aycock and Leonard George Goss

Appendix A

WRITING ARTICLES

WRITING ARTICLES

The focus of this book has been upon books and how to write them. We realize, however, that many of you reading this guide are interested in writing material other than books, such as articles and curriculum. With this fact in mind, we offer several items for your consideration about writing non-book material.

Remember that everything discussed up to this point related to the mechanics of writing and querying still holds true. You must be neat, organized, and write an interesting and sensible query letter. Remember, every query you send out is nothing less than a job application. So be careful with it.

In his book *Freelance Writing: Advice From the Pros*, Curtis Casewit points out that people read articles in magazines in order to improve themselves, to confirm their own beliefs, to exercise their minds, to have something to talk about, and to use the material in their own work.[1] All these reasons, and others, will motivate people to read *your* articles.

But where do writers get ideas for articles? Casewit gives several clues: reading; listening to people; utilizing life experiences, even the painful ones; becoming angry at someone or something and deciding to do something about it; talking to editors; scanning public relation or publicity material; watching television or listening to the radio.[2] Reviewing chapter 2 of this book will also help.

In the space which follows, I (DMA) want to show you some of the actual articles I have had published and examine what went into the writing of them, what prompted them, and what I was hoping to accomplish. These are certainly not master-pieces of article technique, but they do serve as learning models.

The Serious Article

One type of article is the straight-forward informational piece, or the "serious" article. This is often the sort of thing found in magazines such as *Newsweek* or the like. In this type of writing the author wants to convey information, to explore a problem, or perhaps to offer a solution. In religious magazines, this type of piece might be found in everything from *Leadership* to *The Christian Century.*

The following article appeared in *Church Administration.*[3] I was serving as pastor in a church which was located close to a funeral home. An unusually large number of people in that community had no church affiliation, so the funeral direc-tor would often call on me to conduct funerals for people I had never met. This presented many problems, especially since I was a young pastor at the time. I researched the situation and tried to find help, but nowhere could I find anything per-tinent to this situation. I realized that if I could write something about it, from my own experience, other pastors might benefit. The article, entitled, "Funeral Ministry Outside the Church," drew favorable response from readers. Remember that one important source of ideas is a problem upon which little or nothing has been written.

Funeral Ministry Outside the Church

DON M. AYCOCK

"Hello Pastor, this is Mr. Morgan at _____ Funeral Home. We just received the body of a woman who lived in your community. Her family tells me she has no present church, but they think she 'used to be' a Baptist. They requested that a Baptist minister handle the service. Can you come right over?"

In my tenure at my present church I have received dozens of such calls. Funeral ministry in general is difficult, but working with people you do not know compounds the problems. My purpose in writing this article is to identify some of those problems and issues and to offer some insights I have gained.

Will I Work With Families I Do Not Know?

Each minister has to answer this question on his/her own. Those who are extremely busy within their own congregation may not wish to get involved. Others may know themselves well enough to refuse to handle funeral ministry if they "freeze" in unfamiliar circumstances.

However you have answered this question in the past, I hope you will periodically review your decision. For me personally this was no real question until after I had done several such funerals. I simply assumed that *any* minister would be glad to help. Only later did I realize that some have policies against it.

The First Meeting With the Family

Once the decision is made to handle the service, the minister's first meeting with the family and/or friends of the deceased is the most important one. It will set the tone and pace of subsequent meetings and interviews. I usually try to plan to meet the family at the funeral home soon after they arrive but before neighbors and others get there. The director usually introduces me and I try to get everyone's name and their relationship to the deceased. I have found it imperative then simply to sit quietly and let the family talk to me. Some will talk about their feelings. Others will review the past accomplishments (or failures) of the one who has died. Sometimes no one talks and the minister may need to use leading questions. I like to use these: "What would you like me to know about your Aunt Suzy?" or "What kind of relationship did you have with her?" There are others, but anything which can help the family open up is useful.

Sometimes well-meaning family members will want to "canonize" their relative, so the minister should be on the lookout for this set up. Others have harbored anger against the relative and might react with a mixture of grief, guilt, and hostility.

Who Is In Charge Here?

Usually during this first meeting with the family, one clear leader will emerge. This is often a woman who is seen as "the strong one." The minister can get much useful information from this person, especially when it comes to planning the service.

It must be remembered that, ultimately, the minister, not the "leader" of the family, is in charge. By this I mean I will not surrender the final outcome to anyone else. Some families have made requests of me which were totally inappropriate, and I gently but firmly had to decline. One wanted me to give a lengthy eulogy, but since I had never even met the deceased I said, "no."

Since these people often have no ties with any church, they are often at a loss to suggest any order of the service or specific elements of it. If "Aunt Suzy" had a favorite Scripture verse or hymn I will try to incorporate it into the service. Do not be surprised, however, if the family can make no suggestions.

Working closely with the funeral director is important here. He or she can be very helpful in making suggestions to the family about matters of the service, appropriate dress, behavior, and so on. I have found that many of the people in my neighborhood, for example, have never even *been* to a funeral before and are at a loss as to how to dress or what to do.

The Minister's Own Emotions

I have never yet ministered at a funeral for the unchurched without feeling ill at ease. The problem is compounded by the often tragic or unusual circumstances surrounding the death. My emotions are touched and I have to work at staying together in order to conduct the service. Consider some of the following examples from my ministry to see how they affect you.

● Mr. P., 72, went for a walk along the Ohio River in Louisville. He died while out there and the body was discovered two days later. It was frozen solid. The exact cause of death was difficult to determine and the family was frantic.

● A six-year-old boy, Chuck, stepped from between two parked cars in front of his house and was struck by a car. He lived four days before dying. His father was so angry he tried to kill the driver of the car. (This happened near Christmas.)

● Mrs. A., 55, died in a nursing home sixty miles from home. Her husband had gotten tired of her because she was bedridden with arthritis. (This man was an alcoholic, practiced bestiality with the family Collie, and would often beat Mrs. A.) So much tension and hatred surfaced over the cause of death that threats and counter threats were made by various members of the family. I demanded that a policeman be present during the service to keep anyone, including me, from getting killed. (This is another example of what I mean when I say that I am in charge.)

● Mrs. L. died at age 108. She was the widow of a Civil War veteran.

● Mrs. D., 57, died. Two of her seven children were in prison. The legal technicalities of release threatened to prevent them from attending their mother's funeral. Only after legal bickering and a story by an investigative reporter from a local paper did the boys get out for the hour of the funeral. They were led into the chapel in handcuffs and chains. Armed guards stood watch during the service.

● An infant of two days died. The family could not afford a funeral so a local mortuary donated a casket, and the family had the infant's grandfather's grave reopened, and the tiny casket placed in it.

All these, and many others, underscore the pain, anger, and bewilderment often felt by people who lose loved ones. The minister is not immune to these feelings, and therefore, he needs to take care not to cave in under the pressure. After the service the minister may need to debrief with some trusted friend or counselor. These loads are often too heavy to carry alone.

To Preach or Not to Preach?
Eulogies are out by virtue of the fact the minister does not know the deceased. Some read from prayer books and follow a set liturgy. I opt for as much personalizing as possible. An overarching view of the family of the deceased can be worked into the meditation if it is done with care. I often hear phrases like, "Uncle Bill was always so generous with everyone,"or "Mother just loved little children," and so on.

I am well aware that some ministers question the use of a funeral meditation at all, especially one based on Scripture and a Christian understanding of reality. For me personally, I cannot extricate myself from my calling as a Christian pastor. That is, I cannot simply, "say a few good words" over the deceased with no reference to God or eternity. I am not a mortician— but a pastor. People realize this fact when they ask me to help in a funeral service.

Follow up
The funeral service is over, the family and friends have gone home, and the minister goes to his/her next appointment. But what about tomorrow? A strong temptation is simply to forget the matter and go on about business as usual. Fight this temptation. These people really are "sheep without a shepherd." A follow up visit in the home can do worlds of good for the bereaved family. I like to visit two or three days after the funeral and give them a copy of the meditation used. They seldom hear it in their grief at the service anyway, and most appreiciate the concern and consideration.

I have found that these unchurched families are not especially good fields for evangelism. Some will respond to the claims of the gospel and become involved in the church, but my experience has shown that most will not. Many have lived all their lives with no meaningful relationship to the church. Even a death in the family will not necessarily send them scurrying to worship. It is best to work with each situation individually.

Summary
When doing funeral ministry with the unchurched, expect the unexpected. Assume nothing . . . and be on the lookout for signs of complete bewilderment in the family. You as the minister, must exercise a compassionate control. Someone must be in charge. ●

What I tried to do in this article was clarify in my own mind what I was called to do in conducting a funeral ministry to families outside the church. I tried to explain the major issues, use actual incidents to illustrate the problems, and offer solutions or suggestions which might help someone in a similar situation.

Devotions

A well-respected form of religious writing is the devotional. This form of writing has been around a long time and looks deceptively simple. But this genre is hard to compose and harder to publish because you must communicate something significant and unique in a short space.

I once had a conversation with the editor of a magazine devoted exclusively to devotional material. She told me that she reads hundreds of devotional articles per year but rejects most because they are trite, stale and generally lack any import. This editor said that many of the devotions she sees are like swamps,—they ooze all over.

This first piece was one in a series I was asked to write for *Family Devotions.*[4] The biblical text was assigned, which can be a problem. I tried to get the readers' attention and then apply the truth of the passage and personalize it for the reader.

He Is The Light

Wednesday, Febraury 11, 1981
*Read:*John 8:12-20

I have visited Mammoth Cave in Kentucky several times. Each time, the guide gives us a "natural" view of the cave, a view of what it looks like without man-made lights. When the lights are turned off, the darkness seems to have texture, to be thick. You can see absolutely nothing. The guide then strikes one match which lights up the whole room in the cave.

That is a parable which helps me to understand Jesus' words, "I am the light of the world." Without him we are "in the dark" concerning a personal relationship with God. With him, we can "see" our way to the Father.

We think in analogies all the time—this is like that. We likewise use analogies in our religious language—"Jesus is like light in the darkness." To say this is to affirm all of the qualities in Jesus which are like light—warmth, security, stability, and lack of fear. It is a truly great day when we can affirm, not only that Jesus is the light of the world, but also, "He is the light of my life."

This second devotion appeared in *The Upper room.*[5] I wrote it when I was feeling "crusted up" spiritually. At that time I ran across a remark Mark Twain once made to a friend, and it seemed like a revelation to me. As I wrote it I felt a kind of cleansing.

Tuesday, October 17, 1978
Read Romans 12:1-12

Let your hope keep you joyful, be patient in your troubles, and pray at all times. -Romans 12:12 (TEV)

Mark Twain once wrote to a friend and advised him to take out his mind and dance on it because it was getting all crusted up. Prayer is something like dancing on one's mind, or breaking away from all of the clutter—worry, fear, anxiety—which cuts us off from an unhindered communication with God.

Jesus certainly took great care never to allow His mind to "crust up." Each prayer cleared the way to the openess of communication which can come only through an unhindered mind.

One way we "dance on our minds" is through periodic inspection of our motives and desires. It is when we have cleared away the bonds which hold us back that we can live openly and joyfully.

***Prayer* O Lord, clear away the crust which shuts us off from open communication with You. We pray as Your Son, our Savior, taught us, "Our Father, who art in heaven . . . Amen."**

Thought For The Day
Our minds, like everything else, need periodic clearing.

Humor

Everyone I know enjoys an amusing piece now and then. I have come to respect anyone who can write good humorous articles. They are tough! Humor is serious business.

While reading my mail one day I opened a package from a mass mailer offering "necessary" items for my ministry. As I thought about some of the items being offered, I could not help but laugh when I imagined actually having some of that paraphernalia. I sat at my typewriter and in about twenty minutes produced the following article. It appeared in a denominational journal, *The Baptist Program.*[6]

Of Mail, Markets, and Mirth

My morning mail brought a brochure full of ads from a company selling "church-oriented" products. As I thumbed through this treasure chest full of obviously "necessary" items, several in particular caught my attention.

The first was a boot-legged fortune cookie. Instead of some fantastic fortune inside, it has a Scripture verse. The ad quoted some minister as saying, "I take them along on hospital visits." They must be for his lunch. How would you like to be hospitalized and have some joker come along and poke a Scripture cookie at you? You wouldn't? Oh well, that's the way the cookie crumbles. . . .

The next thing I saw was the ad for a 75-plus-year-old set of "handy homiletical helps." (How's that for preacher jargon?) I think the subtitle was "Simple Sermons for Simple Preachers." This is just what every pastor needs. Communication is so hard already, what more harm could the language, illustrations, and thought patterns of 75 years ago do? (I ordered three sets to give to my minister friends of other denominations. What a great way to cut down on the competition!)

The next little gem was an absolute must for us—protection for our stained glass windows. The problem is that our windows are stained by the rust caused by water dripping on them from the coping above, and by the traces of the mud balls the kids threw up there during the last rain. But why spend good money to protect these windows? They are getting more stained all the time. They don't need help.

The one I really liked had the caption, "Raise Funds: Sell Trash. . . ." Visions of dollar bills danced in my mind as I looked out at our parking lot and spotted a broken Pepsi bottle, three crushed beer cans, a shredded paper who-knows-what, and the back seat of a 1957 Buick. My euphoria was short lived, however, as I re-read this ad and saw the word ". . . Bags" on the next line.

Three ads tried to make me order new cushions for our pews. What a perfect idea. If we bought them I could brag at the next minister's luncheon how I really filled up every pew in my church. Again my plan was thwarted when I realized how many of our people carry permanent cushions. I never have had the nerve to ask anyone if his or hers was "reversible and nonslip."

There were lots of other goodies in the brochure. We could get a badge-making kit and print cute lapel pins. For only two dollars we could get information on mortgages and loans, but we're so broke we don't have two dollars. I could get 1,000 cassettes so my members could "hear the pastor's sermon again and again." Who are they trying to kid?

If we ordered the custom-made, three-high nursery crib, I would have a great object lesson for the text, "Be fruitful and multiply." I would get some of those cute little earphones for the hard of hearing only if they come with *no*"off" switch.

Some of my fellow ministers cringe when the mailman leaves these little brochures for them. But I don't. It's one way to insure my day will not pass without a good laugh.

Signs on the old railroad crossings used to read, "Stop, Look, Listen." That is exactly what the writer of humor must do. Humor at its best comes out of observation. My friend, the late Grady Nutt, used to say that real life was a hundred times more funny than imagined situations. And Grady was a genius at observing the little absurdities in life and pointing them out with wonderful results.

Personal Opinion Articles

An article which is relatively easy to write is the personal opinion piece. It is exactly what the name implies—one person's opinion about something. Anyone could write this sort of article.

The first article below is one which I wrote when I first entered seminary. My experience was different from what I expected, so I expressed some of my frustration in writing. The seminary I attended reprinted the article in a brochure which was sent to all prospective students.[7]

Impressions of life at a seminary by a currently enrolled student. It's not exactly heaven on earth; neither is it all doom and gloom.

SEMINARY CAMPUSES AND BARE FEET

"Then he said, 'Do not come near; put off your shoes from your feet, for the place on which you are standing is holy'." Exodus 3:5, R.S.V.

Many well-meaning people envision a seminary as a place where everyone walks around barefooted! To them, the seminary is a small piece of heaven on earth, a place where angels continually sing and God is ever present. Naturally, those who hold this view of a seminary never attended one!

Those of us currently enrolled in a seminary have a quite different view. Continually bombarded from every side by new ideas and new pressures, many of us feel as though we could never be "put together" again by "all the king's horses and all the king's men" (or by anything else). This situation sometimes leads to frustrations, fears, and disappointments.

Prospective students need to better understand what life on a seminary campus is really like. By taking some positive steps before entering a seminary, a student may avoid some of the disillusionments.

Contrary to popular belief, a seminary is not isolated from the rest of the world. Seminary students have the regular everyday experiences of life—from paying bills to changing dirty diapers. The students know firsthand problems and strife just as do residents in the community surrounding the school.

Many students find a seminary somewhat dull in comparison to the college or university they have just left. It's not because there's nothing to do—in fact, there's almost too much to be done. But the atmosphere is different. Unlike college, a seminary does not continuously offer activities. There are no football or basketball teams, except for intramurals. Extracurricular activities are at a minimum. The fact is, most seminary students are too busy in their graduate work to support such activities even if they were available.

Students who make their way into seminary are usually well educated and highly motivated. All have graduated from a college. Competition for grades at the seminary level is keen. The pressure to succeed and get good grades is too great for some. Incidents of cheating and dishonesty, although rare, do occur even in a seminary context. Other students just drop out. Some are made bitter by the pressure, and repercussions are evident throughout their lives.

In the face of stiff competition, and perhaps tougher grading policies, a student must make up his mind to apply himself diligently and be willing to let the grades take care of themselves.

Another type of pressure felt by most students entering seminary is theological pressure. Most come to seminary with preconceived ideas. Then they are introduced to Barth, Bultmann, Bonhoeffer and Tillich, Whitehead, von Rad, and an endless list of other thinkers. Some of their notions may be badly shaken.

The answer to the problem is an understanding that seminaries exist to build faith with knowledge, *not* to destroy faith. New ideas will be presented and old ones examined closely. But above all, a seminary never intends to jeopardize one's personal relation to Christ. Students who go to seminary with an open mind and a trust in Jesus will discover other matters will eventually fall into their proper places.

Finances are a real "thorn in the flesh" to many students. Southern Baptists have provided ministers with an opportunity for a high quality education with their gifts through the Cooperative Program and endowments. This education is available to students at a comparatively low cost.

Even so, it is often hard to make ends meet. Some students are trying to repay money borrowed to attend college while furthering their education in seminary. Many wives of students work. Churches and other organizations provide some assistance and scholarships. Still, money is tight. The cost of books is enormous. The time that a student can work is limited by his academic load. Financial pressure can become a real detriment to a student's efficiency in school.

A realization that this situation will not last forever helps. After graduation, financial conditions usually improve. Also, some churches do pay student ministers quite well.

Trying to be a minister while in seminary can be a real source of depression and disillusionment. There never seems to be enough time to get everything done. Trying to be a student and a minister at the same time is like trying to hold two full-time jobs. Other students are never able to find the real situations for ministry that they desire while in seminary.

A student coming to a seminary needs to understand that some opportunity for ministry will present itself. It may or may not be what is specifically desired. But God has something for everyone. The type of ministry which presents itself may not be easy, but all the while, it may help a young minister learn and grow.

Just because I have focused attention on some of the problems of seminary life does not mean all is doom and gloom. Far from it. But by frankly anticipating some of the real life problems, new students can help their days at the seminary be truly a time of spiritual and intellectual growth.

The second article was one I wrote when I was feeling dissatisfied with my preaching ministry. It actually began with one idea, and ended up as another because I changed my mind during the writing process. This article appeared in *The Western Recorder* and was simply my own idea about where I was at that time.[8]

Perfunctory Preaching: IOU To Congregations

This article began as "Confessions of a Pulpit Prostitute." I imagine many other pastors are like me. They mount their pulpits on Sunday mornings, ready or not. They speak words, but not always the Word. It seems to me, or at least it seemed, to do this constitutes the prostitution of one's calling, using it for impure motives.

As I thought through this matter I changed my mind. I am not trying to salve my conscience or to condone sloppy and ill-prepared work. What happened was I looked closely at the faces which greet me when I rise to preach on Sunday morning.

On my left is a middle-aged woman whose life seems mortally boring. Behind her a man who is continually struggling to grow up. To my right sits an older man who has fought the demon alcohol all of his life. Often he loses the battles. Behind me in the choir is a lady in her late 80's. She realizes life for her is almost over. Next to her is a teenaged boy who is trying to find his place in life.

The point is all of these people bring with them great needs. They need a word from God to lift them up, assure them, strengthen them and prepare them for life now and the life to come. I have to ask myself, "What right do I have not to feed these people when they come to church? When they come seeking bread, can I give them a stone in the form of a weak excuse for having no bread?" I realize my concern for not having what I consider to be the exact word for them is a form of pride. Who am I to know exactly what they need? Only God can know. Through my words, however prepared. He speaks to this people. Even my shabbiest efforts are sometimes blessed of God.

I have no right to withhold God's blessing from my people simply because I do not feel inspired. The gospel does not primarily rest on how I or other preachers feel. It stands on the power and purpose of God himself.

"Perfunctory preaching" can be thought of as perhaps mechanical or without feeling. But by this term I mean preaching which is done, without regard to how I feel, or what the weather is like, or how large the crowd is, or anything else. It is a plea for steady, week by week preaching which is the best that can be done on any given Sunday. Paul admonished Timothy, ". . . proclaim the message, press it home on all occasions, convenient or inconvenient . . . " If we can follow Paul's advice and are faithful, then we have the opportunity to see God's promise unfold before our eyes. "My word will not return onto me void."

Article with a Unique Format

A useful thing to remember is that the printed page can give the author a unique format with which to express a thought. You have seen the following sign which utilizes both a message in words and a message in logistics:

You can use the printed page to your advantage if you plan your work in advance. I once wanted to write something about church committee members who did not take their work seriously. One way to do so was to simply berate them, but that is not the most effective method to change behavior. What I did was use a format which was itself the message. Read the following article to see if you get my point.[9]

You Really Don't Count?

The First Baptist Church was a pleasant little place. It was what most people would call a "model" church. Everyone got along well.

The budget was in good shape, and all of the committees functioned smoothly.

In fact, the committees worked *too* smoothly! Because things went so well, the members began to feel that they were not *really* necessary.

One day things began to change. One committee member said, "I have so many other things to do, I'll just drop out of nry place of responsibility. The church is so full of capable people, I won't even be missed." So he dropped out of his committee.

The next week anather parson thought, "If I dan't continue in my pesition in the church, who will knaw?" So he, too, gaze up his jod.

Then onx morx member dacided to gize up hes share of the resqonsibility in the charch. This ment thet anothxr person had ta do doubly duty.

A thurd mezber gaze up his jod, and threo othxrs hed to werk threx thmez as hard.

Thdn a foxth qzit, and a fivtk, and siyth, too!

Tzis onty gaes ta prxve one fyct: is yay are a mendar of a cyurch comnittex, yau *really* dzn't cawnt!

This brief article was used by a bulletin service which circulated it to one and a half million people. Afterwards, it was reprinted several times by magazines and individual churches.

Parable

We are all aware of how effectively Jesus used parables. But have you ever thought about writing one for yourself? Several books of modern parables exist today which might give you a clue about how to write them. Check your local library.

I wrote a little parable about a flying pulpit which appeared several years ago in *Pulpit Digest*.[10]

NIGHTMARE

We moved along at a safe enough speed but at an altitude I thought was too low. "Hey, who's in control of this thing? A Boy Scout?" I asked a nearby stewardess.

"Sir," she remarked sternly, "The pilot's name is Captain Whim, and the co-pilot's name is Lieutenant Popularity."

"What? That's the craziest thing I ever heard! We don't even seem to be on course. Where are we heading?" I asked.

"Oh, just whichever way the wind is blowing," replied the attendant nonchalantly.

She could tell I was getting worried when I said, "Whoever heard of such a thing? I demand to speak to the pilot."

"Certainly, sir, just as soon as we take a survey to see whether or not we will be keeping him."

"Then I demand my money back."

"Sorry, sir, but don't you remember? You spent nothing at all to enter this craft."

"When are we going to land?"

"Oh, whenever."

"How are we going to land?"

"Sometimes we come right in for a smooth touchdown but not too often. Many times we just go around and around in circles until we almost land. Then just as all the passengers are about to unbuckle their seatbelts—swoosh!—we're back in the air. Sometimes we land so quickly the passengers don't even know we took off. Once in a while we just fly around until we run out of gas. Then we have to crash land. But what really makes the passengers mad is when we finally touch down, and then taxi up and down the runway for a long time for no apparent reason. But you know, even after the most bumpy of flights, some folks insist on saying to the pilot, 'I sure did enjoy the flight today'."

I sat up in bed, turned on the light, and wiped the sweat from my brow. Only then did I realize I had dreamed of taking a flight in my own pulpit.

Parables have a way of inviting a reader to accompany the writer on a journey, but at a safe distance. Just when the reader thinks he is most safe, the writer can then "set the hook," making his point in an unforgettable way.

The How-To Article

One of the most popular kinds of articles today is the "how-to." In this type of article the author tells the reader how to do or think about something.

Stop and think how many things you could teach someone else. The number is probably greater than you realize. Listing some of the things you are good at or at which you have a lot of knowledge might give you ideas for many saleable articles.

I once wrote a "how-to" piece for *Christian Writers Newsletter*.[11] This article was "How To Write a Book In Ten Easy Steps." I began by telling my readers *never* to believe a title such as the one on the article they were reading!

HOW TO WRITE A BOOK IN TEN EASY STEPS

So you want to write a book? You are to be commended for the courage to compete with the 45,000 plus other people who will publish books next year. You may be among those would-be writers who could well produce a publishable book manuscript if you had just a little help. That is what this article is all about. Let me offer a few suggestions.

1. **Never believe a title such as the one on this article.**

   There are *no* "ten easy steps" or "six simple lessons" for writing a book. Writing is hard work and if you are not willing to accept that fact, you might as well give up your book writing desires. However, there are a few guidelines you might want to keep in mind as you peck away at the typewriter.

2. **Clarify in your own mind exactly what the central theme of your book is.**

   If you cannot state your theme in one sentence, you probably have not thought it through sufficiently. For example, you would not want to write a book on, "Family Life." That is too broad a topic. Clarify it. Ask yourself questions to narrow the focus and theme. What aspect of family life do you want to concentrate on? How is your book going to differ from others on the same subject? Choosing a particular angle is necessary, such as "The Christian Family: A Futurist Perspective."

3. **Learn to use language creatively.**

   I am not talking here about just the basics of grammar, but about the creative use of words. Train yourself to think creatively. The imagination, like other mental faculties, can be trained and developed. If you are interested, send me a self-addressed, stamped envelope (a SASE), and I will send you a bibliography of books on creativity and imagination. The use of your imagination will raise your writing from the ranks of the unpublished to the realm of published.

4. Research your topic.

Most books, whatever the topic, benefit from thorough research. The purpose of this is not just to give facts and figures, but also a new perspective. Writers are like honeybees, collecting nectar from various flowers in order to make honey. Writers are generally not like spiders which spin their webs from their own insides. One suggestion: If you have need of a well-stocked theological library, but do not live close to one, write the Congregational Library, 14 Beacon Street, Boston, MA 02108 and ask to be put on their mailing list. They lend books free of charge and will send you brochures periodically listing their recent acquisitions.

5. Adopt a professional attitude toward your writing.

By "professional" I do not mean that you will earn all your living from writing. Instead, I have in mind the need to be businesslike and efficient in your writing and in your dealings with publishers. This includes such matters as neatly typing your work, addressing query letters to the appropriate editors, keeping careful records, avoiding over-zealous letters to the editor on the merits of your work. (If it is good, he will find out for himself.) Accept rejection of your work gracefully, but do not give up. Send out another query the very next day. If you believe in your work, show it. Stick with it until some publisher wants it.

6. Study the markets carefully.

Know the kinds of materials various publishers handle. Sending a book which attacks tongue speaking, for example, to a Pentecostal publishing house is both foolish and a waste of time. An agent may be helpful in this area. They know the markets well and are able to guide your manuscript to the appropriate places.

7. Work, work, work.

You cannot rely on "inspiration" alone in book writing. Inspiration can get you going but determination and sweat will keep you going. Writing, after all, is the art of applying the seat of your pants to the seat of your chair. Remember this little poem—cut it out and tape it to your desk or typewriter:

Sitting still and wishing,
Makes no person great.
The good Lord sends the fishing,
But you must dig the bait.

That's only seven suggestions, not ten after all. I hope they help. May
your mailbox be filled with acceptance letters and your heart with joy.
Happy writing!

Paraphrase

Another good way to communicate is to write a paraphrase
of some well-known item. You are probably familiar with
Kenneth Taylor's paraphrase of the Bible known as *The Living
Bible*. That version is not a translation closely following the
original Hebrew and Greek Scriptures, but a free rendering
in the author's own words what he understands the Scriptures
to say.

You can do something similar with a portion of Scripture,
for instance. Chapter 1 of this book ends with Marian
Forschler's paraphrase of I Corinthians 13 for writers.

A couple of years before I had seen that paraphrase, I used
this same passage for a word to my fellow preachers. I wrote
it especially for ministers in my own denomination and used
names in the paraphrase which would be immediately
recognized by them.[12]

I Corinthians 13 For Preachers

Even if I speak with the eloquence of G. Earl Guinn or the thunder
of Bailey Smith, if I have no love I'm merely tooting my own horn.
If I have the gift of preaching like Wayne Ward and can fathom all
mysteries like John Newport, and if I have faith like R.G. Lee, even
enough to move mountains, if I have no love I'm still a zero. If I
give away all I make, like W.A.Criswell, or become a martyr, like
Ralph Elliott, if I don't love I will not have gained an inch on heaven.

Love gives latitude and is genuinely kind. It isn't pretty or pom-
pous or proud. Love is gracious and selfless. Love keeps its temper
and doesn't keep a log of wrongs. It isn't proud of evil but it is ecstatic
in the truth. Love always shields, always trusts, always believes the
truth in the face of the obvious, and always hangs in there.

Love never poops out. All preaching will cease, languages will become tongue-tied, and knowledge will fade from memory. We all have our blinders and speak only partial truth. But when the real thing appears, all imposters will be exposed. When I was a kid I jabbered like a kid, thought childishly, and reasoned illogically. But when I grew up I left Tinker-toy thinking far behind. Now we see truth as if it were reflected in a warped mirror; then we will see it eyeball to eyeball. Now I know only fragments; then I will have the whole picture, even as my true self will be fully comprehended.

Now these three things hold on: faith, hope, and love. But the *summon bonum* is love.

Try your hand at this sort of writing. You may find it as fun as it is challenging.

Sermon

Some of you reading this book are ministers who preach regularly. Have you considered publishing your sermons? Most pastors do not write sermons specifically for publication, but you might find that if you do write sermons to be preached in your church, they could do double duty with some careful rearrangement. *Pulpit Digest* and *Vital Sermons of the Day* publish many sermons by ministers from many denominations. Since you might not be familiar with these publications, let me give you their addresses. *Pulpit Digest* may be reached by writing the editor, Dr. James W. Cox, 2825 Lexington Road, Louisville, KY 40280. The address of *Vital Sermons of the Day* is 6116 East 32nd Street, Tulsa, OK 74135.

The following sermon example appeared in *Pulpit Digest*.[13] I wrote it for delivery to my congregation, and only after it was preached did I send it for possible publication.

UNVEILING THE MYSTERY OF GOD

Text: Romans 16:25-27

Imagine yourself standing in a crowd waiting for the unveiling of a famous statue. The dignitaries are in place; the band has a drum roll; and the moment of removing the veil arrives. But a problem arises—the cover will not come off. The crowd sighs almost in unison and breaks up as people begin wandering off. That would be an embarassing moment.

Now shift the scene a bit. Imagine that, instead of a statue under the veil, it is God. When we try to unveil God we find that the cover is also tight. John Oman once said that four veils hide the mystery of God from men. Those veils are ignorance, sin, weakness, and mortality. Oman suggested that each of these covers is removed by some aspect of Christian faith.

Ignorance is removed by the incarnation. The proclamation of Christmas is far more than a once-a-year remembrance. It is a gospel for the whole year. It is "Immanuel" "God with us." This is a thought so incredible that many laugh at it. But the Bible teaches us that God became man and lived the life of a human. We read in John's gospel,"The Word became flesh and lived for a while among us"(1:14). Jesus told his disciples, "Anyone who has seen me has seen the Father"(John 14:9).

In a real sense we are all ignorant of God. No one has ever seen Him. Plato once said that people can't find out anything about God, and even if they could, it would be impossible to tell anyone else about Him. Many people are not so much anti-religious as simply non-religious; they are agnostics rather than atheists. Some are serious seekers of truth, but they can't seem to get a handle on God. A little girl was put to bed in a dark room. When she protested, her well-meaning mother said, "Now dear, don't worry. God is with you." The little girl countered, "Maybe, but I want someone with a face."

We all want "someone with a face." Most of us don't do so well when we think of God as "the ground of Being," as the philosophers put it. But when we can put a face with Him, when we can think of God as the Father of Jesus, we can think of Him as one who loves us.

So the doctrine of the incarnation removes the veil of ignorance. While we cannot totally know God we can at least know His intentions. We look at the life, work, death, and resurrection of Jesus and see in it the outline of the Creator of the world. We hear his words, "I came to seek and to save those who were lost," and we see a heart.

This perspective will revolutionize our Bible study. When we read the New Testament as God's biography rather than as a compilation of ancient legal documents, then Bible study becomes more meaningful. It will also revolutionize our relationship with other people. Because we realize that God is not unknowable we can talk with other people about Him and his love.

Sin is removed by the atonement. When theologians were seeking for a way to explain the way that God relates to men, they had to come up with a new word. That word is "atonement" and it literally means "at-one-ment." Through Jesus Christ we are at one with God. But how are we to understand this? The New Testament has various models to explain it. The apostle Peter spoke of atonement as the dawning of a new age in a futuristic setting. Jesus, he felt, had inaugurated the new age of forgiveness.

Paul had a different model. He spoke of the atonement as justification in a legal setting. Paul was a zealous Jew who thought in legal terms. He felt that men needed to be declared "not guilty" before God. He said that what Jesus did was to put us in good standing with God. We couldn't do it for ourselves, so God provided Christ to be our defending attorney, so to speak. In Christ "we make bail." So the legal model was used by Paul to explain the atonement. He spoke of it in Romans 5:8-9:"But God shows his love for us in that while we were yet sinners Christ died for us. Since therefore, we are now justified by this blood, much more shall we be saved by him from the wrath of God."

Different models emerged after the New Testament was written. But the point was the same, people had an experience with Christ that changed their lives. We still have that experience. Various interpretations of that experience help us to understand it, but it is the experience and not the interpretation that is important. Because of Jesus, our relationship with God has changed.

Sin is basically an attitude and a relationship. As an attitude it shifts our thinking and our devotion from God to ourselves. As a relationship sin interrupts our communion with God and other people. But what Jesus did on the cross changes that when we trust him.

The cross speaks to us of suffering, and suffering is the most universal of human experiences. If Jesus was willing to take a cross, was he not willing to straighten out our selfish attitudes and interrupted relationship with God? Could we say that Jesus was something like a marriage counselor between us and God? We can use that model only if we say that we, not God, caused the problem to begin with.

Helplessness is removed by the gift of grace. We sing of the wonderful goodness of God's grace, but what do we mean? We mean that God does something for us that we cannot do for ourselves. I went hunting once and became entangled in a barbed wire fence. I could not free myself. Every time I moved the barbs would stick me. A hunting companion had to free me. That was like grace.

Carroll Wise is a well-known professor of pastoral care and a chaplain. Several years ago a water heater exploded and scalded him. Dr. Wise woke up in an intensive care unit of a hospital with third-degree burns over one-third of his body. He was told that the shock to his system had weakened his heart and because of that he could do nothing for himself except press a button to summon a nurse. That was total weakness and helplessness. Grace was the doctors and nurses doing for him what he could not do for himself.

God's grace is like that. We already know much of our

weakness. About all we can do is press a button to summon help. How? We do it by calling out to God, "Lord, I cannot control myself. I cannot save myself. Will you do it for me?" The miracle of grace is that he does it.

A well-known painter decided to capture street scenes of London on canvas. He searched for a boy of the streets, and found an urchin dressed in rags but who had a great deal of sharpness. The boy was to represent all such boys in the painting. The artist told the boy to come as he was to his studio at 9 a.m., and he would paint him. At 9 a.m. sharp the painter's housekeeper ushered a little boy into the studio. His face was scrubbed, his hair was brushed, and his ragged clothes cleaned and sewn as well as possible. "Who are you?" demanded the artist. "Don't you remember, sir? You told me yesterday that you would pay me to come here and let you paint me." The artist shot back, "But I wanted you just like you were. If you had come as you were I would have paid you. But now I will not have you!"

The grace of God says to us, "Come as you are." Isaiah told the people of his day, "Your righteousness is as filthy rags," and so it is with us. We cannot become good enough or clean enough on our own. "Come as you are" is still God's invitation.

Mortality is removed by immortality. Second Timothy 1:10 reads, "(This grace) has now been revealed through the appearing of our Savior Christ Jesus, who has destroyed death and has brought life and immortality to light through the gospel." These words strip death of its terror and its power to paralyze us with fear. It is a strange irony that some people fear death so much they cannot enjoy life. But the gospel speaks directly to this situation and gives measureless comfort. An inscription on the Allegheny Observatory at the University of Pittsburgh reads, "We have loved the stars too fondly to be afraid of night." Isn't that what our gospel tells us? We love God too fondly to be afraid of the night.

A man visited his doctor. The kindly old doctor told him that he had an incurable illness. He asked the doctor what the future life would be like. About that time the patient's dog who had come with him began scratching at the door. The doctor said, "I can tell you this. It's similar to what your dog is showing us. He doesn't know what is in here, but he does know that his master is here."

We don't know what lies behind death's door, but we do know that our Master waits for us there. If we are only cheap candles blown out at death, or mere drops of water absorbed into oceans of being, then we are earth's most pitiful creatures. But Christ has broken the fangs of death and we need not fear it's bite, for whatever it brings, it will be for our betterment.

These four veils, ignorance, sin, weakness, and mortality, hide the mystery of God from us. But each is met and overcome by the power of God. We are too spiritually blind to see all of God, but we catch a glimpse in Christ. Won't you allow Christ to show God to you?

Book Reviews

Do you like to read current books? If so, then you might want to consider writing book reviews. Local newspapers, denominational journals, and religious magazines all use reviews of books which are current and of interest to their readership.

Ask yourself questions about the book you hope to review which you would like answered if you were reading a review of that book: Who is the author? What are his or her qualifications for writing the book? What is the overall theme or message of the book? Who would profit from reading the book (if anyone)? Are there any weaknesses in the work? If so, what are they? And so on.

The following two samples are reviews I wrote for *Reformed Review*.[14] More often than not, a journal will contact a reviewer and ask for a review of specified length. Such was the case here. I have also contacted editors of publications I think might review a particular book I have read to see if they would be interested in my evaluation. (By the way, since I have been on both sides of the book review writing, I have learned to be more kind!)

Be Brief About It, by Robert D. Young, Philadelphia: Westminster Press, 1980, 144 p.,$5.95.

As the title indicates, this is a book about developing a style for preparing shorter sermons. Many preachers think they must fill a half hour on Sunday morning with their sermons. Young argues, however, that preachers should trim their sermons down to shorter times— twenty, fifteen, or even ten minutes.

He is not advocating simply lopping off a point or two on an outline. Rather, he asks the reader to begin developing an entire style of brevity. To support his position, Young offers three reasons for doing so.

First, the mood of the times requires a brief, terse style. Modern America is on the run. Thus, the effective preacher will style his or her sermon to capture the attention of these fast movers and then make the gospel point. Second, theology sanctions brevity. Jesus himself mastered the art of brevity. His parables, for example, display the way a point can be made quickly and powerfully. As Young puts it, " . . . long theological statement betrays its subject. It deadens, while professing that its subject is the God of life" (p.33). And third, contagious communication utilizes brevity. "Long sermons invite dawdling." "When a long time slot is the first consideration, we are tempted to forage for suitable material. But reverse this. Having found a vast topic, vital to faith, force the topic down to fit a ten-or fifteen-minute time slot. Use economy of language, picturesque phrases, short sentences, rapid transitions, a rough-cast ending"(pp.40-41).

Young offers ten guidelines for accomplishing his goals. (1) Think small. (2) Adopt a poetry model. (3) Select a simple unity. (4) stay close to the original inspiration. (5) Make the point quickly. (6) Trim the cast. (7) Time's up—sign off! (8) Take soundings. (9) Feel comfortable with silence. (10) Let the listener do the traveling.

A third section of the book ponders the question,"Does brevity compromise anything in the Gospel?" Young feels it does not. A fourth section contains four brief sermons in which the author puts his theory into practice.

Robert D. Young, who is Senior Pastor of the Westminster Presbyterian Church of West Chester, Pennsylvania, has offered provocative views on preaching. Any preacher could profit from a careful reading of this book. I am tempted to be verbose about this book on brevity! But I will stop by saying it stimulated my thinking, and I consider any book which does that exciting.

*Preaching is Dialogue: A Concise Introduction to Homiletics,*by Henry J. Eggold, Grand Rapids: Baker Book House, 1980. 124 p., $5.95.

The sub-title of this book accurately describes its subject matter. This is a "concise" introduction, not to the wider realm of homiletics, but to a specific approach to preaching. Dr. Eggold, who is Professor of Pastoral Ministry and Homiletics at Concordia Theological Seminary in Fort Wayne, Indiana, helps the reader develop a particular way of viewing the task of preaching. That way is dialogue.

The first three chapters lay the foundation for the remaining seven. Eggold argues that a preacher today must be keenly aware of the process of communication. The communication of the Word of God via preaching is best served by dialogue, which allows for the give and take between preacher and congregation.

Chapter four examines the two foci of the preaching message: Law and Gospel. Both must be held in balance lest the sermon degenerate into moralizing or pious palaver. Eggold concludes that a good sermon is theocentric, kerygmatic, eschatological, and existential (p.48).

Chapters five through nine seek to explicate the practical implications of what has gone before. Suggestions on listening dialogically to the text, of developing a dialogical style of writing, and of delivery are given here.

Chapter ten places the sermon within the context of worship.

Individual worship services are to be viewed within the wider context of the Christian year. This helps the preacher to do both short and long-range planning of sermons.

Preaching is Dialogue is not distinguished by its originality. Eggold has sprinkled the text with quotations of various lengths from some of the standard works in the field of preaching. These are distracting at times.

This book will not teach a student how to write a dialogue sermon, in the common sense of that word. It will, however, help him develop a healthy understanding of what the task of preaching is all about. That factor, above any practical advice which might be had, makes *Preaching is Dialogue* well worth reading.

Compilation Article

Let me mention one other category of article you might try. This is what I call the compilation article. In this type of writing the author compiles a list of items on a certain subject for a specific reason. I recently saw an article in a newspaper on 60 ways businesses can say "no" to an employee's new ideas on ways to improve the business. That was a compilation article.

I once put together a list of fifteen proverbs from various sources in a compilation article published in *Proclaim*, a journal for preachers.[15] The proverbs were intended for use as sermon illustrations.

Proverbs to Live By

The following proverbs, which make excellent one-line illustrations, are taken from *Proverbs to Live By*, published in 1968 by Hallmark Cards of Kansas City, Missouri.

A book whose sale is forbidden all men rush to see, and prohibition turns one reader into three.—Italian proverb

Four things come not back—the spoken word, the sped arrow, the past life, and the neglected opportunity.—Arabian proverb

An empty vessel makes the greatest sound.—Shakespeare

A lie has no legs, but scandalous wings.—Japanese proverb

Conscience gets a lot of credit that belongs to cold feet.—Anonymous

As long as the sun shines, one does not ask for the moon.—Russian proverb

The fall of a leaf is a whisper to the living.—Russian proverb

Once you have missed the first buttonhole, you'll never button up.—Goethe

Perfection is attained by slow degrees; it requires the hands of time.—Voltaire

Thank not those faithful who praise all thy words and actions, but those who kindly reprove thy faults.

He who sacrifices his conscience to ambition burns a picture to obtain the ashes.—Chinese proverb

Think of going out before you enter.—Arabian proverb

Asking costs little.—Italian proverb

The wise man has long ears, big eyes, and a short tongue.—Russian proverb

If a man could have half his wishes, he would double his troubles.—Franklin

What kind of compilations could you come up with to help others?

Summary

I have listed eleven types of articles or kinds of writing in this section. These include the serious article, devotions, humorous pieces, personal opinion articles, articles with unusual formats, parables, how-to articles, paraphrases, sermons, book reviews, and compilation articles. This list certainly does not exhaust the various kinds of non-book writing which can be done. Use your imagination and experiment with these types, along with others you may find or invent. The world of publishing is always on the lookout for a word creatively written.

NOTES

1. Curtis Casewit, *Freelance Writing: Advice From the Pros* (New York: Collier Books, 1974),p.65.

2. Ibid., pp.83ff

3. From *Church Administration*, December 1981. Used by permission, Sunday School Board, Southern Baptist Convention. Copyright 1981. All rights reserved.

4. From *Family Devotions*, January-February 1981. Used by permission, C.S.S. Publishing Co.

5. From *The Upper Room*, October 17, 1978. Used by permission, The Upper Room, 1908 Grand Avenue, Nashville, TN 37203.

6. From *The Baptist Program*, April 1980. Used by permission, Executive Committee, Southern Baptist Convention.

7. From *The Baptist Program*, August 1975. Used by permission, Executive Committee, Southern Baptist Convention.

8. From *The Western Recorder*, May 23, 1979.

9. From *Baptist Bulletin Service*, February 22, 1976. Used by permission.

10. From *Pulpit Digest*, March-April 1981. Used by permission.

11. From *Christian Writer's Newsletter*, July 1982. Used by permission, *Christian Writer's Newsletter*, 300 East 34th Street, (9C), New York, NY 10016.

12. From *Proclaim*, January-March 1984. The Sunday School Board, Southern Baptist Convention.

13. From *Pulpit Digest*, September-October 1982. Used by permission.

14. From *Reformed Review*, Fall 1981, and Spring 1981. Used by permission.

15. From *Proclaim*, October-December 1979. Used by permission.

Appendix B
WRITING CURRICULUM

WRITING CURRICULUM

Anyone who has ever attended Sunday school is familiar with the study materials used in most classes—curriculum. Some people have the mistaken idea that Sunday school classes are random studies of the Bible. They certainly are Bible studies, but they are not random—at least they shouldn't be.

Wesley Tracy teaches writing courses for Christian publications at Nazarene Theological Seminary in Kansas City, Missouri. Tracy writes, "Sunday school is not random study of the Bible and Christian belief. Millions of dollars are spent on developing Sunday school curricula. Various denominations and publishers develop precise educational outlines for all age groups."[1] Tracy goes on to note that one of the "hungriest" markets for writing today is that for the take-home papers distributed in Sunday school classes. Yet many good writers fail to sell to these markets because they fail to understand that any one element is but one part of a "curriculum family" that governs the overall editorial content. That "family" might include study books, teacher's books, specific teaching aids, filmstrips, cassette tapes on some facet of the lesson, magazine articles which tie in with a particular lesson, and so on.

Herb Montgomery worked as the curriculum director for Winston Press for a number of years. He assesses the curriculum field as follows:

The creation of a basic curriculum is an enormous task because it deals with such a wide range of age levels. Preparing materials for toddlers is quite different from developing a program for the elementary grades or a course of study for high schoolers. Yet, each level has to be conceived, outlined, researched, and written. The editorial work involved is rather like the assembling of a thousand-piece jigsaw puzzle. Everything interlocks horizontally and vertically. That is, the year-long sixth-grade program with its series of thematically related lessons must flow smoothly out of the fifth-grade and into the seventh-grade program.[2]

Curriculum publishers usually organize and operate on a three-to-five year plan, but some may even have a ten year plan. This is why they make specific assignments rather than simply accepting whatever free-lance work which might be sent their way.

Montgomery says that the rewards of this type of writing vary greatly. The creator of a simple film-strip might be paid several hundred dollars, while a person who creates a whole range of material in one educational package might get as much as one hundred thousand dollars in royalties. Our experience in writing curriculum and in talking with other writers shows that the former figure is far more realistic than the latter.

The Curriculum Difference

Some have wondered how curriculum differs from the writing of a book. The best explanation of that difference has been given in a paper by curriculum editor Ernest L. Hollaway.[3] Hollaway talked about the five distinctives of curriculum writing:

1. Curriculum is designed to achieve well-defined and predetermined educational objectives.

2. Curriculum materials are to be prepared within the frame of reference given by the designer and are to interpret designated content in a manner that will enable the user to achieve the objectives set.

3. Curriculum materials must be written to relatively exact

specifications as to length, readability level, completion date, and style.

4. Curriculum materials usually are prepared for an audience whose general characteristics have been identified and whose knowledge and/or skill in a subject is at least partially understood.

5. Curriculum materials usually are prepared separately for the leader and the member, and these two separate pieces must be properly related.

Hollaway notes that these distinctives are sometimes seen as limitations which restrict the writer. But a better way to see the five distinctives would be as channels through which the writer can discipline his efforts and send his message to an audience eagerly waiting to read what he writes.

Broad Guidelines

Each publisher of curriculum has its own sheet of guidelines for its material. We list here some broad guidelines for consideration by the curriculum writer:

1. A Sunday school quarterly is primarily an *aid to learning.* The writer does not simply share his own discoveries of the Bible's meaning, but writes in such a way as to help the reader discover and apply the truths of the Bible. Thus, *discovery learning* is the goal.

2. A writer must make a *thorough* study of the Bible passages of topics to be covered. This will prevent presenting shallow views or expositions.

3. The outlines the publisher provides the writer are developed for a purpose and should be followed closely. Often particular lessons are part of a larger unit with definite learning goals. Those goals govern the overall style and content of the individual lessons.

4. The "unit approach" should be kept in mind as the writing proceeds.

5. Style is just as important in curriculum writing as it is in book writing. This material must *grab and hold the attention* of the reader, as with any other kind of writing. As Halford

Luccock once observed, "We have a moral obligation to be interesting." The material should be life-centered. Living language is better than heavy theological jargon. The writer should not be afraid of emotion or personal conviction. Since Bible study is more than a merely intellectual exercise, personal faith and feelings may shine through. Indeed, they really *must* shine through. Curriculum writers, too, are trying to share the Good News.

Getting It On Paper

Once a curriculum assignment has been given to a writer, a question still remains: "How do I get it all down on paper?" Writing curriculum is like any other kind of writing in that the writer must translate concepts and ideas into concrete words. D.P. Brooks, an editor with the Sunday School Board of the Southern Baptist Convention, has a 13-item checklist for getting the curriculum assignment on paper:

1. Picture the entire assignment, relating each part to the whole.
2. Take a close look at each session and sketch ideas regarding sources, ideas, methods, art, sketches, and so on.
3. Make a separate file for each session and watch for materials that fit.
4. Do intensive scholarly research and note taking.
5. Examine the outcome in light of your study and decide on the purpose and the approach you will take.
6. Structure the session material with an outline showing basic content and structure the introduction, Bible study, and so on.
7. Collect any additional materials that will be needed: analogies, case studies, quotations, statistics, etc.
8. Write out a rough draft to the approximate specifications.
9. Go over it carefully to evaluate the structure, progression, clarity, age group slant, balance, variety, literary quality.
10. Rewrite and polish until you are satisfied with the copy.
11. Read it to someone, or have someone read it, and give some feedback to you. Make any needed clarification or correction.
12. Mail to your editor on schedule and be prepared to do a rewrite if required.

13. Keep a copy of all materials in your files until the lessons are in print.[4]

Perhaps this checklist will be helpful as you think about all kinds of writing, including curriculum assignments. Can you think of other items which should be on the list?

The Writers' Conference

Some publishers of curriculum require the writer to attend specially-designed conferences. For example, the Southern Baptist Convention requires that their curriculum writers attend such a conference. The main facets of such conferences are detailed below. You may find this helpful if you ever attend such a meeting.

The conference might last two afternoons and two full days. On the first evening, after the writers arrive and check into the motel where the conference is held, there is usually a banquet and then a group session on the specific kinds of curriculum writing they will be doing.

The next morning all those writing biblical content materials would meet in one room, and those writing methodologies in another for an overview session. That afternoon there might be a general session on writing. The evening could be spent in meetings with all writers from the specific quarters together. The following morning and afternoon would be spent in the same kinds of meetings, the writers working on a specific quarter's material gathering to "brainstorm" and study. A resource person would lead but everyone is encouraged to contribute their ideas.

Time is usually spent working with the editors who give useful information about what they have in mind concerning both content and format. The conferences end in a closing session with all the writers attending.

Not all publishers have these conferences, of course. But the ones you can attend are invaluable because you will begin to see how the curriculum "jigsaw puzzle" fits together. The outcome of one such session was an eleven-lesson unit one of the authors wrote on James and I John under the lesson title, "Keys to Christian Living." The *Young Adult Bible Study* for which he wrote had a circulation of 340,000. Many writers of books never see exposure like that.

If you are interested in doing this sort of writing, contact a publisher and explain your interest. This is by no means "easy" writing, but it is rewarding. Listed below are publishers of curriculum material.

Curriculum Publishers

The following publishers produce curriculum materials. Editors at many of these companies told us the same thing: "Have the prospective writer contact us and discuss a proposal before submitting any curriculum samples." That is a good rule of thumb for all of these publishers. Some use free-lance materials, while others do not. Some use writers only from their own denomination, while others cross denominational boundaries. Some of these houses are general curriculum publishers affiliated with no denomination. If writing curriculum interests you, correspond with an editor for the age group you have in mind and discuss your ideas and qualifications. You might just get an assignment.

ACCENT PUBLICATIONS
12100 West Sixth Avenue
Denver, CO 80215

ADVOCATE PRESS
P.O. Box 98
Franklin Springs, GA 30639-0098

ALDERSGATE GRADED CURRICULUM
P.O. Box 2000
Marion, IN 46952

ARBUTA HOUSE
P. O. Box 48
Abington, PA 19001

AUGSBURG PUBLISHING HOUSE
426 South Fifth Street
Minneapolis, MN 55415

BOARD OF DISCIPLESHIP/GRADED PRESS
201 Eighth Avenue, South
Nashville, TN 37202

CHRISTIAN EDUCATION PUBLISHERS
7348 Trade Street
San Diego, CA 92121

CONCORDIA PUBLISHING HOUSE
3558 S. Jefferson
St. Louis, MO 63116

DAVID C. COOK PUBLISHING CO.
850 North Grove Avenue
Elgin, IL 60120

GOSPEL LIGHT
110 W. Broadway
Glendale, CA 91204

GOSPEL PUBLISHING HOUSE
1445 Booneville
Springfield, MO 65802

JUDSON PRESS
Valley Forge, PA 19481

MESSENGER PUBLISHING HOUSE
P.O. Box 850
Joplin, MO 64801

NAZARENE PUBLISHING HOUSE
6401 The Paseo
Kansas City, MO 64131

PACIFIC PRESS
1350 Villa Street
Mountain View, CA 94040

PAULIST PRESS
1865 Broadway
New York, NY 10023

REGULAR BAPTIST PRESS
1300 North Meacham Road
Schaumburg, IL 60195

REVIEW AND HERALD PUBLISHING ASSOCIATION
6856 Eastern Avenue, N.W.
Washington, DC 20012

ROD AND STAFF PUBLISHERS
Crockett, KY 41413

ROPER PRESS
915 Dragon Street
Dallas, TX 75207

SCRIPTURE PRESS
1825 College Avenue
Wheaton, IL 60187

SERENDIPITY, INC.
2550 West Main Street
P. O. Box 1012
Littleton, CO 80160

STANDARD PUBLISHING COMPANY
8121 Hamilton Avenue
Cincinnati, OH 45231

SUNDAY SCHOOL BOARD OF THE SOUTHERN BAPTIST CONVENTION
127 Ninth Avenue, North
Nashville, TN 37234

SWEET PUBLISHING COMPANY
7434 Tower
Ft. Worth, TX 76118

UNION GOSPEL PRESS
P.O. Box 6059
Cleveland, OH 44101

WINSTON PRESS
430 Oak Grove
Minneapolis, MN 55403

NOTES

1. Wesley Tracy, "Outlines for Success in the Religious Market," *Writer's Digest*, March 1981, p. 30.

2. Herb Montgomery, "Writing Christian Curriculum," in *Writing to Inspire*, edited by William Gentz (Cincinnati, Ohio: Writer's Digest Books, 1982), p. 229.

3. Ernest L. Hollaway, "Curriculum: A Different Kind of Writing." This unpublished paper is given to writers of Southern Baptist Convention curriculum.

4. D. P. Brooks, "Getting It On Paper." This is an unpublished paper given to writers of Southern Baptist Convention curriculum.

Appendix C

The Mott Stylebook: A Guide for Authors, Editors and Proofreaders in the Preparation of Manuscripts

THE MOTT STYLEBOOK: A GUIDE FOR AUTHORS, EDITORS AND PROOFREADERS IN THE PREPARATION OF MANUSCRIPTS

The Mott Stylebook

This guide has been prepared by the editors of Mott Media, Inc., Publishers, and is based on *The Chicago Manual of Style*, the 13th Edition Revised and Expanded 1982 by The University of Chicago Press. All topics are cross-referenced with *The Chicago Manual of Style* so additional information and examples can be readily found. However, in the few instances that may be ambiguous, the house style set forth in this book predominates. In publishing this manual, it is our goal to give careful attention to the language and thus communicate effectively with our readership.

—Leonard George Goss
Senior Editor

I.Book Production

Preparation of the Manuscript (2.3-50; 13.17-40)

1. It is the author's responsibility to provide copy that is clear, readable and accurate. The manuscript must be typed and double-spaced. It should have wide margins (1 inch) on good-quality standard white bond paper 8½ × 11 inches. Colored paper or onion skin is not acceptable. Use only one side of the sheet.

2. The manuscript must be complete. Both additions and corrections are confusing and difficult to add once the manuscript has been accepted for publication. The author should include the following parts with the book:
   Title Page
   Table of Contents
   All Text Matter
   Footnotes on separate pages
   Tables or graphs on separate pages
   Bibliography
   Index (prepared by author after page proofs are available)

3. The manuscript pages should be numbered consecutively in the upper *right* corner. The author should *not* number them by chapter (3-1, 3-2, etc.). Sheets inserted after the manuscript has been paginated should carry the preceding page number with *a, b, c* added: 86*a*, 86*b*, 86*c*. If a page is later removed, the preceding page should be double numbered: 106-107.

4. It is the author's responsibility to check all Scripture references and footnotes for accuracy.

Rights and Permissions (4.1-4.59)

1. The publisher will prepare the copyright page and also has the privilege to give permission to reprint excerpts in other publications.

2. If the author wishes to use a portion of a copyrighted work and there is some question whether the kind or amount

of the material exceeds a fair use, permission should be requested. It is the author's responsibility to obtain permission to quote from other sources. Notice of the original copyright and permission to reprint must appear either on the copyright page of the book or in a footnote on the first page of the reprinted material or in a special list of acknowledgments. All permissions or copies of them must be sent to the publisher.

3. The author is further responsible for any fees charged by grantors of permission unless other arrangements are made by the author. When the publisher pays the cost of procuring permission rights, these costs are generally deducted from the author's future royalties.

4. Frequent use of modern Scripture versions may require permission.

Stages in Manuscript Production (2.125; 3.4-5; 3.36; 3.49)

1. An edited manuscript usually passes through the following eight stages in the production process:

   Sample page and design
   Typesetting
   First proofs (copy sent to author)
   Final proofs
   Camera copy
   Platemaking
   Press
   Binding

2. Once page proofs are made, revisions are costly and should be minimal. Major changes at this stage in production are not acceptable. Corrections should be confined to substantive errors.

3. Authors will receive final proofs *only* if the book requires an index. In this case, the author will receive a deadline to complete the index, but manuscript revisions are not made at this time.

II. Punctuation

The Period (5.6-5.12)

1. Use a period without parentheses after numerals or letters in a vertical listing.

   1.
   2.
   3.

2. Numerals or letters in a list within a paragraph should be enclosed in parentheses and should not be followed by a period.

3. Omit the period after running heads, centered headlines and signatures.

4. Periods should be placed within quotation marks except when single quotation marks are used to set off special terms.

   The editor stated that the period "should go inside the quotation mark."

Exclamation Point (5.13-5.15)

1. Use the exclamation point to mark an emphatic or sarcastic comment.

   Watch out!

   What a twit!

2. The exclamation point should be placed within quotation marks, parentheses, or brackets when it is part of the quoted or parenthetical material; otherwise, it should be placed outside.

   "Leave Smokey alone," cried David, "he's my dog!"

Question Mark (5.16-5.23)

1. The question mark is used to pose a question or to express an editorial doubt.

   Shall I come with you?

   The next ruler over the Franks was Charlemagne (742?-814), son of Pepin the Short.

2. Questions which consist of single words, such as *who, when, how,* or *why,* do not require a question mark. It is better to italicize the word.

> The question is not *how* but *when.*

3. The question mark should be placed inside quotation marks, parentheses, or brackets when it is part of the quoted or parenthetical material.

> "Why wouldn't something like that work in Detroit?"

The Comma (5.24-5.67)

A comma is used to indicate the smallest pause in continuity of thought or sentence structure. The modern practice is to pause infrequently, especially if the meaning is clear without an interruption. Aside from a few set rules, its use is a matter of good judgment.

1. Use a comma before the conjunction uniting two parts of a compound sentence unless both parts are very short:

> An Olympic winner receives no money, but the crown of laurels is the greatest honor a citizen can earn.

2. An adjectival phrase or clause that is nonrestrictive and could be dropped without changing the reference of the noun is set off by commas.

> King Louis IX of France, a just and peace-loving man, was called St. Louis by his people.

3. Use commas to set off interjecting transitional adverbs and similar elements that effect a distinct break in the continuity of thought.

> All the test animals, therefore, were reexamined.

4. A word, phrase, or clause in apposition to a noun is usually set off by commas.

> My wife, Carolyn, wrote to our congressman.

However, if the appositive has a restrictive function, it is not set off by commas.

> My son Joseph was the first in his class to answer the question.

5. Two or more adjectives should be set off by commas if each modifies the noun alone.

Beth has proved a faithful, sincere friend.
However, if the first adjective modifies the idea expressed
by the combination of the second adjective and the noun,
no comma is needed.

An angry black tiger was in his path.

6. In a series of three or more elements, place a comma before
the conjunction.

According to legend, Vladimir studied Islam, Judaism,
and Roman Catholicism before deciding to become
a Christian.

7. Use commas to set off words identifying a title or position
after a name.

Nero, the cruel and bloodthirsty emperor who
murdered Christians, was also responsible for the
burning of Rome.

8. Commas must be used to indicate the date.

October 6, 1966 but 6 October 1966

9. A direct quotation or maxim should usually be separated
from the rest of the sentence by commas.

"I am afraid," said Martin, "that I can offer no
explanation."

However, if the quote is restrictive appositive, or used as
the subject or predicate nominative, it should not be set
off with commas.

"Under no circumstances" was the reply he least
expected.

The Semicolon (5.68-5.73)

A semicolon marks a more important break in sentence flow
than one marked by a comma.

1. Use a semicolon between two independent clauses not con-
nected by a conjunction.

The controversial portrait was removed from the entrance hall; in its place hung a realistic landscape.

2. The following adverbs—then, however, thus, hence,
indeed, yet, so—should be preceded by a semicolon when
used between clauses for a compound sentence.

Mildred says she intends to go to Europe this summer; yet she makes no definite plans.

3. Use a semicolon to separate a compound sentence when either part of the sentence has a comma break.

David is a well-trained, talented artist; and he is always tempermental.

4. Semicolons may be used for emphasis.

It was the best of times; it was the worst of times.

5. Semicolons should be used to separate references when they contain internal punctuation.

Genesis 2:3-6 ; 3:15, 17; 6:5, 9, 14.

The Colon (5.74-5.81)

A colon marks a discontinuity of grammatical construction greater than that indicated by a semicolon, but less than a period. Its one main function is to introduce material that follows immediately.

1. A colon may be used to emphasize a sequence in thought between two clauses that form a single sentence.

Some of the policemen worked two jobs: twelve of them, for example, worked as guards at night.

2. A colon may introduce a list or series.

Binghamton's study included the three most critical areas: McBurney Point, Rockland, and Effingham.

If, however, the series is introduced by *namely, for instance, for example,* or *that is*, a colon should not be used unless the series consists of one or more grammatical complete clauses.

3. A colon should be used between chapter and verse in Scripture passages.

Matthew 2: 5 - 13

The Dash (5.82-5.96)

1. An endash is used to indicate inclusive or continuing numbers, as in dates, page references or Scripture references.

1970-80

Jan-June 1982
Mark 4:3-6:12
pp. 30-42

2. The emdash (—) denotes an abrupt break in thought that affects sentence structure.

> The emperor—he had been awake half the night waiting in vain for a reply—came down to breakfast in an angry mood.

3. A two-emdash (no space on either side) indicates missing letters.

> We ha——a copy in the library.

4. A three-emdash (with space on each side) indicates a whole word has been omitted.

> The ship left ——— in May . . .

Quotations (10.1-10.35)

1. Direct quotations must reproduce exactly in the wording, spelling and punctuation of the original. However, the initial letter may be changed to a capital or lowercase letter to fit the syntax of the text. Typographical errors may be corrected in modern works, but idiosyncrasies of spelling in older works should be observed.
2. It is the author's responsibility to check every quotation against the original for accuracy.
3. Quotations over eight lines are set in block quotes. Shorter quotations may be set in with the text.
4. If the quotation, either run into or set off from the text, is used as part of the author's sentence, it begins with a lower-case letter, even though the original is a complete sentence and begins with a capital letter.
5. Direct conversation, whether run into or set off from the text, should always be enclosed in quotation marks.
6. Quoted material set off from the text as a block quotation should not be enclosed in quotation marks. Quoted material within a block quotation should be enclosed in double quotation marks, even if the source used single quotation marks.

7. Scripture used in block quotations must be followed by the reference in parentheses.
8. The words *yes* and *no* should not be quoted except in direct discourse.

   > Joshua always answered yes; he could not say no.

Parentheses (5.97-5.101)

1. Parentheses, like commas and dashes, may be used to set off amplifying, explanatory, or digressive elements. Commas, however, should be used if the two parts are closely related.

   > He had long suspected that the inert gasses (helium, neon, argon, krypton) could be used to produce a similar effect.

2. Expressions such as *that is, namely, e.g., i.e.,* and the element introduced, may be enclosed in parentheses if the break in thought is greater than that signaled by a comma.

   > Bones from several animals (e.g., a dog, a cat, a squirrel, a pigeon) were found in the grave.

3. Parentheses should be used to enclose numerals or letters marking divisions or enumerations run into the text.

   > The anthropologist stated there were no inexplicable differences between (1) Java man, (2) Neanderthal man, and, (3) Cro-Magnon man.

4. Ending punctuation should be placed outside a closing parenthesis if the word or phrase in the parentheses interrupts or is interjected into a sentence. However, when a question mark or an exclamation point is part of the parenthetical matter, it may precede the closing parenthesis.

   > A consistent format should be followed (do not punctuate by ear).

5. Ending punctuation is enclosed in parenthetical matter which is an entire sentence independent of another context.

   > Was this a desperate cry for help? (Or any one of a hundred other considerations?)

6. When quoting Scripture, place the period after the parenthesis containing the reference. If the quotation requires

a question mark or exclamation point, place it with the text, and place the period after the parenthesis.

> "In the beginning God created the heaven and the earth" (Genesis 1:1).

> "Lord, are you going to wash my feet?" (John 13:6).

Brackets (5.102-5.106)

Brackets enclose editorial interpolations, corrections, explanations or comments.

> She [Susanna Wesley] died in 1742, leaving her children a rich heritage.

Brackets may also be used to enclose the phonetic transcript of a word.

> He attributed the light to the phenomenon called gegenschein [ga - gen - shin].

Ellipses (10.36-10.49)

1. Any omission of a word, phrase, line or paragraph from a quoted passage must be indicated by ellipsis points.
2. Three dots . . . indicate that material is deleted at the beginning of or within a sentence.

   > "By faith Moses' parents hid him for three months . . . because they saw he was no ordinary child" (Hebrews 11:23).

3. Other punctuation may be used on either side of the three ellipsis dots if it makes the meaning clearer.
4. Three dots may indicate a break in thought, daydreaming, or hesitation. But a dash should be used to indicate an *external* interruption of speech or thought.

   > If he had only come sooner . . . if only . . . then perhaps everything would have been different. I - that is, we - yes, we wish he had come sooner.

5. Unless the content requires such, it is not usually necessary to use ellipsis points before or after a verse or a portion of a Scripture verse.

   Introductory words such as *and* and *for* may be omitted from a Scripture quotation without ellipsis points.

"For God so loved the world . . ." (John 3:16) may read "God so loved the world . . .".

6. Four dots . . . . indicate that material is omitted at the end of a sentence (the extra dot accounts for the period). The missing material could be (1) the last part of a quoted sentence (2) the first part of the next sentence (3) a whole sentence or more (4) a whole paragraph or more.

    "All the believers were together and had everything in common. . . . Everyday they continued to meet together" (Acts 2:44, 46).

    If the original quotation is punctuated with a question mark or an exclamation point, this mark is retained and the three dots used for the ellipsis:

    "Now is my soul troubled; and what shall I say? . . . for this cause came I unto this hour (John 12:27).

The Apostrophe (6.5 - 6.23)

1. The apostrophe is the mark of the possessive. The possessive case of singular nouns is formed by the addition of an apostrophe and an s, and the possessive of plural nouns by the addition of an apostrophe only.

    the book's cover
    the puppies' tails

2. When it can be done without confusion, numbers and letters used as words form the plural by adding s alone.

    the three Rs
    four YMCAs
    early 1930s

3. However, abbreviations with periods, lower case letters used as nouns and some capital letters may require an apostrophe for clarity.

    M.A.'s
    Ph.D.'s
    x's and y's
    S's, A's, I's

4. The general rule for common nouns is also used for proper

names, including most names of any length ending in sibilants.

Peter's boat

Cheryl's baby

Rosses' house

Burns's poems

Exceptions: the names Jesus and Moses are traditional exceptions to the general rule for forming the possessive.

Jesus' disciples

Moses' staff

III. Spelling and Proper Use of Words

Italics (6.52-53; 6.61; 10.52-53)

1. The author may underline a word or phrase to emphasize it with italics.
2. Technical terms, especially when accompanied by definition, may be set in italics the first time they appear.

    Tabular matter is copy, usually consisting of figures, that is set in columns.
3. Isolated words or phrases in a foreign language should be italicized.

    ad lib

    au revoir

    sine gua non
4. A person's thought, in contrast to verbal discourse, may be set in italics for clarity.
5. References to words as words are italicized.

    The word *faith* has often been confused with hope.

Hyphenation (6.24-47)

1. Hyphens are to be used cautiously. Most compound words do not require a hyphen. Most noun combinations which were formerly hyphenated are now written as solid words: butterfat, willpower. Others are still hyphenated: well-being. Some that were once hyphenated are now two

words: water supply. Keep a copy of *Webster's Seventh New Collegiate Dictionary* on hand so as not to hyphenate by intuition.

2. A word or phrase used as an adjective is often hyphenated.
   born-again Christian
   soul-winning program
   born again (noun)
   Soulwinning was . . . (noun)
3. For further clarification, *The Chicago Manual of Style* pp. 176-181 should be consulted.

References (15.58-66)
1. Footnotes should be numbered consecutively throughout each chapter of the book.
2. Footnotes should be typed on sheets separate from the text, be double-spaced and have generous margins.
3. Notes will usually be printed at the end of the chapter or the end of the book. The decision will be made by the editor.
4. Each footnote should include the following information:
   Author's full name
   Complete title of book
   Editor, compiler, or translator, if any
   Edition, if other than the first
   Number of volumes
   Facts of publication - city where published, publisher, date of publication
   Volume number (if any)
   Page number(s) of the particular citation
5. When citing an article from a periodical as the source, the following information should be given:
   Author's full name
   Title of the article
   Name of the periodical
   Volume (and number) of the periodical
   Date of the volume or issue
   Page number(s) of the particular citation

6. After the first reference to a particular work in each chapter, subsequent references in the same chapter should be shortened. The shortened reference should include only the last name of the author and the short title of the book, in italics, followed by the page numbers of the reference.

> 1. Jerrold J. Katz, *The Philosophy of Language* (New York: Harper & Row, 1966), p. 42.
>
> 2. J. Stevenson, *The Catacombs: Rediscovered Monuments of Early Christianity* (London: Thames and Hudson Ltd., 1978), p. 159.
>
> 3. Katz, *Philosophy of Language*, p. 73.

7. "Ibid." may be used to refer to a single work cited in the note immediately preceeding. It takes the place of the author's name, the title of the work, and the succeeding identical material.

> 1. Ronald H. Nash, *Social Justice and the Christian Church* (Milford, Mi.: Mott Media, Inc., Publishers, 1983), p. 75.
>
> 2. Ibid., p. 153.

8. It is the author's responsibility to provide complete and accurate footnotes.

Scripture References (7.84-87; 14.33-35; 17.63)

It is the author's responsibility to provide accurate and complete references to the Bible.

1. Books of the Bible should not be abbreviated when the reference is cited without chapter and verse.

2. In block quotations, the names of Bible books may be properly abbreviated.

3. Arabic numerals will be used to cite all references to Scripture.

> 2 Chronicles
>
> 2 Peter
>
> 3 Peter

4. The names of Bible versions may be abbreviated when citing a reference. (See abbreviations)

5. When quoting Scripture, place the period after the parenthesis containing the reference. If the quotation ends in a question or exclamation point, place it with the text and place a period after the parenthesis.

   "Finally, my brethren, rejoice in the Lord" (Phil.3:1).
   "Jesus saith unto him, If I will that he tarry till I come, what is that to thee?" (John 21:21).

Abbreviations (14.1 - 14.56)

1. Abbreviations should not be used for given names.
   William not Wm.

2. When a civil or military title is used with the surname alone, the title must be spelled out.

   General Washington
   Lieutenant Daly

   If the full name is used, however, the title may be abbreviated.

   Sen. Everett M. Dirksen

3. Abbreviations are always used for Mr., Mrs., or Dr.

4. The names of government agencies, organizations, associations, and other groups may be abbreviated. Such abbreviations are usually set in capitals without periods.

   NATO
   TV

   The same applies to famous persons known by their initials only.

   FDR
   RFK

5. The names of states, territories, and possessions of the United States should always be spelled out when standing alone.

6. The names of countries, except for the Soviet Union (often abbreviated USSR), are spelled out in the text.

7. Names of the months should be spelled out in text, whether alone or in dates. They may be abbreviated in chronologies or footnotes.

Jan.	July
Feb.	Aug.
Mar.	Sept.
Apr.	Oct.
May	Nov.
June	Dec.

8. The days of the week should be spelled out.
9. Parts of a book may be abbreviated for use in footnotes or bibliographies.

appendix	app.
book	bk.
figure	fig.
folio	fol.
note (s)	n. (pl. nn.)
number	no.
page (s)	p. (pl. pp.)
paragraph	par.
volume	vol. (pl. vols.)

Abbreviations and Scripture References (7.84; 14.33-35; 17.63)

1. In text, references to whole books of the Bible or whole chapters are spelled out.

> The opening chapters of Ephesians . . .
> Genesis, chapters 1 and 2, records the creation of the world.

2. Biblical references may be appreviated when enclosed in parentheses. In some scholarly or reference works, they may be abbreviated in the text.

Gen.	2 Sam.	Ps. (pl. Pss.)
Exod.	1 Kings	Prov.
Lev.	2 Kings	Eccles.
Num.	1 Chron.	Song of Sol.
Deut.	2 Chron	Isa.
Josh.	Ezra	Jer.
Judg.	Neh.	Lam.
Ruth	Esther	Ezek.
1 Sam	Job	Dan

Hos.	Jon.	Zeph.
Joel	Mic.	Hag.
Amos	Nah.	Zech.
Obad.	Hab.	Mal.

New Testament

Matt.	Eph.	Heb.
Mark	Phil.	James
Luke	Col.	1 Peter
John	1 Thess.	2 Peter
Acts	2 Thess.	1 John
Rom.	1 Tim.	2 John
1 Cor.	2 Tim.	3 John
2 Cor.	Titus	Jude
Gal.	Philem.	Rev.

Books of the Bible should be referred to with the title used in the version cited. For example, Song of Solomon is Song of Songs in *The New International Version* and not abbreviated.

3. Arabic numerals are used for all references. If the reference begins a sentence, the number should be written out.

      1 John   First John 3:16 says . . .

4. Versions of Scripture may be abbreviated in references and set in small caps without periods.

AV	Authorized (King James) Version
RV	Revised Version
NEB	New English Bible
ASV	American Standard Version
JB	Jerusalem Bible
LB	Living Bible
MLB	Modern Language Bible/New Berkeley
NASB	New American Standard Bible
NIV	New International Version
RSV	Revised Standard Version
Phillips	
Amplified	

5. The abbreviation for *verse* is v. and for *verses*, vv.
   v. 23
   vv. 24-26

IV. Use of Numbers in Text

General Rules for Numbers in Text (8.2-8.76)

1. If the word following the number is not a measurement, numbers under 10 are written as words and numbers 10 and over are written as numerals.
   Our two computers are kept busy 24 hours a day.
2. Exact numbers of less than one hundred and round numbers in hundreds, thousands or millions should be spelled out.
   Thirty children . . .
   four billion
   3.6 billion
   2,486
   124
3. Two exceptions to this rule are year numbers and numbers referring to parts of the book.
   43 B.C.   page 6
4. Initial numbers at the beginning of a sentence should be spelled out.
   One hundred fifty . . .
   Twenty-five percent . . .
5. When numbers precede units of measurement, they are written as numerals and the units may be abbreviated.
   3 cubic inches
   63 pounds
   10 lb.
   22 ft.
   6 gal.
   10 percent
   60 volts
   34° *F.*
   5 hr.

6. Numbers applicable to the same category should be consistent throughout a paragraph. If the largest number contains three or more digits, use figures for all.
7. Where there are two adjacent numbers, spell out one of them.

> sixty 12-in. rulers
> 100 twenty-cent stamps

8. Use a period without parentheses after numbers in a vertical listing.

> 1.
> 2.
> 3.

9. Numerals in a list within a paragraph should be enclosed in parentheses and should not be followed by a period.

Currency (8.23-29)
1. Isolated references to money in United States currency are spelled out or written in figures according to general rules for numbers.

> give dollars
> Each employee received $36.10 for wages, $10.36 for benefits and $2.10 for cost-of-living.

2. Substitute million and billion for zeros, but use zeros for sums in thousands.

> $6 million
> $10,000

Dates and Times (8.33-49)
1. Spell out (lowercase letters) references to particular centuries and decades.

> nineteenth century   but 1940s
> sixties and seventies

2. Dates should be consistently written in one of the following forms. Never use st, nd, rd, or th after figures in dates.

> 19 October 1954
> *Saturday Review*, 5 October 1968, p.26
> The third of June, 1943
> June 5 (never June 5th)

3. Times of day are usually spelled out in the text.
   > The church meeting wasn't over until four-thirty.

   However, figures may be used to emphasize the exact time.
   > The train arrived at 3:20.
4. Figures are used in designations of time with A.M. or P.M.
   > 4:00 P.M.
   > 3:25 A.M.
5. House numbers or street addresses are given in figures.
   > 814 Forest
   > Interstate 90

   However: Fifth Avenue
6. In figures of one thousand or more, commas should be used between every group of three digits.
   > 46,324
   > 1,314

   Exceptions to this rule are page numbers, addresses, and year numbers of four digits, which are written in figures without commas.

V. Capitalization

Titles and Offices (7.15-26)

1. Civil, military, religious and professional titles are capitalized when they immediately precede a personal name.
   > President McKinley
   > General Patton
   > Emperor Maximilian
   > Queen Elizabeth
2. In text matter, titles following a personal name or used alone in place of a name are, with few exceptions, lowercased.
   > Abraham Lincoln, president of the United States
   > President Lincoln, the president of the United States
   > the president, presidential, presidency
   > General Ulysses S. Grant, commander in chief of the Union army

General Grant
the commander in chief
the general
George VI, king of England
the king of England, the king
the bishop of London
Clyde M. Haverstick, Doctor of Law
John Snider, M.D.

Kinship Names (7.30)

A kinship name is lowercased when not followed by a given name, even in direct address or when the term is substituted for a personal name.

his father
my brothers and sister
Uncle Charlie
Aunt Sara
Mother's middle name is Marie.

Political Divisions (7.34-37; 7.54-56)

In general, words designating political divisions of the world, a country, state, city and so forth are capitalized when following the name or an accepted part of it.

Roman Empire; the empire under Augustus; the empire
Washington State; the state of Washington

Organizations (7.47-58)

1. Names of national and international organizations, movements and alliances and members of political parties are capitalized, but not the words *party, movement, platform* and so forth.

   Communist party; Communist(s); Communist bloc
   Common Market
   Loyalist(s)
   Republican party, platform; republican(s)
2. Nouns and adjectives designating political and economic systems of thought and their proponents are lowercased, unless derived from a proper noun.

        bolshevism
        communism
        democracy
3. Words derived from personal or geographical names are
    lowercased when used with a specialized meaning.
        dutch oven
        french fries
        india ink

Holidays and Seasons (7.31; 7.71-72)
1. The four seasons are lowercased except when personified.
2. The names of religious holidays and seasons are capitalized.
        Christmas Eve
        Easter Day
        Pentecost
        Passover
3. Secular holidays and other specially designated days are
    also capitalized.
        Fourth of July; the Fourth
        Mother's Day
        Thanksgiving Day

Capitalization of Religious Terms (7.20; 7.74-92)
1. The names of the one supreme God are capitalized.
        God
        Adonai
        Logos
        Jehovah
        the Word
        Redeemer
        Yahweh
        the Savior
        Master
        Son
        Holy Spirit
        Christ
2. Pronouns referring to God are capitalized to eliminate

ambiguity in passages containing other pronouns but not capitalized if the text does not require such added clarity.

Trust in Him.

God gives man what He wants.

Jesus and his disciples.

3. Though the names of specific places in Scripture are normally capitalized, *heaven, hell* and *hades* are lowercased.
4. Use lower case for biblical events, incidents or periods, except for future days of reckoning.

    ascension
    atonement
    birth
    coronation
    creation, the
    Day of Atonement
    Day of Judgment
    death
    exodus, the
    flood, the
    incarnation
    nativity
    resurrection
    temptation

    Exception: Capitalize adjectives derived from proper names, e.g., Mosaic dispensation; Christian era; Maccabean period; Messianic age.
5. The following list of biblical and religious terms are capitalized or lowercased according to house style:

Advent, the	apostle Peter et al.
Advent season	apostles
Almighty, the	Apostles' Creed
almighty God, the	archangel
angel	ark, the (Noah's)
ante-Nicene fathers	ark of the covenant
Antichrist, the	ascension, the
anti-Christian	atheism
Apocrypha, the	atonement, the
Apostle Paul	baby Jesus

Battle of Armageddon
Beast, the (Antichrist)
Beatitudes, the
Bible school
biblical
body of Christ (the church)
Book, the (Bible)
Book of Genesis et al.
Book of the Law
Bread of Life (Bible or
   Christ)
Bridegroom, the (Christ)
bride of Christ (the church)
Calvary
Canon, the (Scripture)
canon of Scripture, the
captivity, the
Catholic church (Roman
   Catholic)
chief priest
children of Israel
Christian
Christlike
Christmas Day
Christmas Eve
church (building, service)
church fathers
Comforter, the (Holy Spirit)
commandment (first, et al.)
Communion
covenant, the
creation, the
Creator, the
Cross, the
crucifixion, the
crucifixion of Christ
Crusades, the
Day of Atonement
Day of Judgment
Dead Sea Scrolls
deism
Deity, the
devil, a

Devil, the (Satan)
disciples
divine
Divinity, the (God)
Easter Day
ecumenism
Eleven, the
end times, the
epistle (John's epistle et al.)
Epistle to the Romans
Epistles, the (apostolic letters)
eternal God, the
eternal life
Evangelicals
exodus, the (from Egypt)
faith, the (Christianity)
Fall, the
fall of man
Fathers, the (church fathers)
Feast of the Passover
flood, the
Fundamentalists
Garden of Eden
Gentile, a
Gethsemane, Garden of
God
godless
godly
Golden Rule, the
Good Friday
Good Samaritan
gospel (John's, et al.)
gospel (adj.)
Gospels, the
hades (hell)
heaven
heavenly Father
hell
High Priest, the (Christ)
high priest, a
Holy Bible
Holy Ghost
Holy Land

Holy of Holies
Holy Scriptures
Holy Spirit
house of the Lord
incarnation, the
Jordan River
  (but river Jordan)
Judaic
judges, the
Judgment Day
kingdom, the
kingdom of God
King of Kings (Christ)
lake of fire
Last Judgment, the
Last Supper
law (opposite of grace)
Law, the (OT)
Masoretic
mercy seat
messianic
Millennium, the
minor prophets (people)
Mount of Transfiguration,
  the
nativity, the
New Covenant
Nicene Creed
Palm Sunday
Passover
Pentateuch
Pentecost
Prodigal Son, the
Promised Land
prophet Isaiah, the
prophets, the (people)
Prophets, the (books of OT)
Protestant (ism)
providence of God
psalm, a
psalmist, the
rapture, the
Reformation

Reformed theology
resurrection, the
resurrection of Christ
Sabbath (day)
Satan
satanic
Savior
scriptural
Scripture (s)
Second Coming, the
second coming of Christ
Sermon on the Mount
Sunday school
synagogue
tabernacle, the (building)
Talmud
temple, the (at Jerusalem)
Ten Commandments
  (but second commandment)
testaments, the
tomb, the
Tower of Babel
transfiguration, the
tribulation, the
Trinity, the
Twelve, the
twelve apostles, the
Twenty-third Psalm
unscriptural
Upper Room, the
Virgin Birth, the
Way, the (Christ)
wise men
Word, the (Bible or Christ)
Word of God (Bible)
Word of Life

Scripture Quotations (10.1-70; 17.63)

Quotations from the Bible should be copied exactly as they appear in the version used, without change in capitalization or punctuation.

Exceptions: When Scripture blocks are quoted in paragraphs, but not versified as in the version quoted, the capitals which were used mostly to distinguish the initial letters of verses should be disregarded.

AUTHOR'S CHECKLIST

_____ Manuscript is typed, double-spaced on white bond with wide margins.

_____ Manuscript is complete and includes:
Title Page
Table of Contents
Text
Footnotes on separate pages
Tables or graphs on separate pages
Bibliography

_____ All Scripture references have been checked for accuracy.

_____ All footnotes have been checked for accuracy.

_____ All quotations have been checked for accuracy.

_____ All notes are complete.

_____ Permission has been granted for quotes from other sources. Copies of the permissions are available for the publisher.

_____ Except for changes made by the editor, the manuscript stands complete and ready for publication.

PROOFREADING AND EDITING MARKS AND EXPLANATIONS

MARK	EXPLANATION	EXAMPLE
e	Take out character indicated.	*e* The prooof.
∧	Left out, insert.	*h* Te proof.
#	Insert space.	# Theproof.
X	Broken letter.	X The proof.
eq.#	Even space.	*eq.#* A good proof.
⌣	Less space.	⌣ The proof.
⌒	Close up; no space.	⌒ The proof.
tr	Transpose.	*tr* A proof good.
wf	Wrong face.	*wf* The *proof*.
lc.	Lower case.	*lc.* The Proof.
sc	Broken scoring.	*sc* The proof.
SC	Solid scoring.	SC The proof
≡ ⊬ ═	Capitals and small caps.	The proof.
caps. ≡	Capitals.	*caps* The proof.
ital caps. ≣	Italic caps.	*ital caps.* The proof.
ital ___	Italic.	*ital.* The proof.
rom.	Roman.	*rom.* The proof.
bf. ∿	Bold face.	*bf* The proof.

stet	Let it stand.	stet The proof.
cc	See copy.	cc ^ He proof.
(sp)	Spell out.	(sp) King (Geo.)
¶	Start paragraph.	¶ read. ¶ The
No ¶	No paragraph; run in.	No ¶ marked. The proof.
⌐¬	Raise.	The proof.
└┘	Lower.	The Proof.
[	Move left.	[The proof.
]	Move right.	The proof.]
‖	Align type.	‖ Three men. Two women.
^ ⊙	Insert period.	⊙/ The proof^
^,	Insert comma.	,/ The proof^
^:	Insert colon.	:/ The proof^
^;	Insert semicolon.	;/ The proof^
V'	Insert apostrophe.	V' The boys arm
V" V"	Insert quotation marks.	V" V" The proof of
=/	Insert hyphen.	=/ A well^known
^9	Insert inferior character.	^9 $A_9 + B_9 = C$^
V9	Insert superior character.	V9 $A^9 + B^9 = C$V
!/	Insert exclamation mark.	!/ Prove it^

?/	Insert question mark.	?/	Is it good∧
Au: ?	Query for author.	? (was)	Proof∧ read by
[/]	Insert brackets.	[/]	∧See Eq. 3(a)∧
(/)	Insert parentheses.	(/)	The proof∧ 1∧
|⅟N|	Insert 1-en dash.	|⅟N|	1922-1958∧
|⅟M| or |⅟M|	Insert 1-em dash.	|⅟M|	A proof.∧ First
|²/M|	Insert 2-em dash.	|²/M|	Taylor∧
□	Indent 1 em	□ The proof.	
⊞	Indent 2 ems	⊞ The proof.	
◪	Indent 1 en (½ em)	◪ The proof.	
] [	Center copy	] The [ ] proof. [	

INDEX

Adair, James, 69, 156
Adkins, Rose, 164
Adler, Bill, 169
Aldleman, Robert, 172
Aldrich, Sandra, 116
Allen, Charles, 73
Alnutt, Frank, 129
Anderson, Becca, 115
Anderson, Margaret J., 165
Anderson, Sherwood, 169
Andrews, Jim, 148
Angione, H., 164
Appelbaum, Judith, 168
Arthur, Donna, 157
Auchincloss, Louis, 173
Auden, W. H., 21, 173
Avallone, Michael, 14
Aycock, Carla, 33n
Aycock, Don M., 33n, 59, 179, 185

Bailey, Herbert S., 163
Bailey, Keith M., 56, 74
Baker, Denys Val, 168
Baldwin, James, 73
Balian, L., 111
Balkin, Richard, 173
Barclay, William, 7-9, 12, 16n
Bartlett, Peter, 144
Barzun, Jacques, 170
Baum, Frank, 73
Belanger, Terry, 164

Beren, Peter, 103n, 164
Berg, Scott, 169
Bermont, Hubert, 167
Berry, Verna, 115
Bettin, John T., 109
Bloom, Ursula, 13
Bogle, Darlene, 116
Bombeck, Erma, 4, 55, 73
Brady, John, 174
Brande, Dorothea, 164
Brohaugh, William, 15n
Brooks, Collin, 7
Brooks, D. P., 214, 219n
Brunson, Evelyn V., 8, 16n, 165
Bryant, Al, 157
Bryant, Jean, 140
Buchwald, Art, 73
Buck, Pearl, 173
Bunnin, Brad, 103n, 164
Burack, Sylvia K., 108, 173
Burke, Patricia, 117

Caldwell, Erskin, 175
Caldwell, Taylor, 169
Calhoun, Ernestine, 110
Campbell, David, 20, 33n
Cantlon, Marie, 131
Cappon, Rene J., 163
Carlisle, Roy M., 64, 138
Carr, Meredith, 128
Casewit, Curtis W., 167, 183, 207n

Ceynar, Marvin, 115
Chenevey, Anthony, 129
Chimento, Norma, 152
Chimsky, Jean, 164
Christie, Agatha, 14
Churchill, Winston, 7-8, 16n
Clark, Bernadine, 174
Clark, Thomas L., 132
Cloete, Stuart, 24, 33n
Coleman, Lyman, 153
Collins, David R., 116
Colvin, Elaine Wright, 16n, 123n, 171
Commins, Dorothy, 172
Commins, Saxe, 172
Connolly, Paul, 110
Cooper, Jack, 116
Corbett, Edward P. J., 169
Coser, Lewis, 165
Cowles, Robert, 135
Cox, James H., 166
Cox, James W., 200
Craig, Tracey Lenton, 166
Crawford, Ted, 103n
Creasey, John, 13
Crim, Keith, 156
Criswell, W. A., 199

Daigh, Ralph, 16n
Davis, Cathy, 133
Dean, Bob, 117
Dennis, Jan P., 137
Dessauer, John P., 164
Dixon, W. MacNeile, 23
Donehoo, Jonathan, 141
Dor, Alexia, 144
Dreiser, Theodore, 172
Drescher, J., 111
Drury, Michael, 174
Dykeman, Wilma, 33n

Eagleson, John, 148
Edgerton, Dorothy, 110

Edison, Thomas, 68
Eggold, Henry J., 205-206
Elbow, Peter, 175
Elliott, Ralph, 199
Ellis, Pierce S., 110
Emerson, Connie, 168
Evans, Glen, 166
Evans, Nancy, 168

Farrar, Larsten D., 171
Farrell, Christopher, 143
Faulkner, William, 172
Fetterman, Bonny, 152
Fitzgerald, F. Scott, 169
Follett, Ken, 108
Folprecht, William, 172
Forschler, Marian Brincken, 14, 16n, 199
Fosdick, Harry Emerson, 10, 12, 16n, 30, 33n, 79, 103n
Foster, Richard, 67
Franklin, Benjamin, 207
Frantz, Phyllis, 142
Franzen, J., 171
French, C. W., 164
Fuhrman, Betty, 57

Gallagher, Nora, 168
Gargiulo, Jack, 53, 64
Garner, Earle Stanley, 13
Gay, Gary R., 115
Gay, Sue, 141
Gearing, Phillip J., 8, 16n, 165
Gentz, William H., 16n, 111, 113, 123n, 171, 175, 219n
Geohegan, Anne, 15n
Gericke, Paul, 34n
Gibbon, Edward, 37, 47n
Gibson, Walter, 13
Gifford, Carey J., 110
Gillquist, Peter, 148
Goethe, Johann W., 207
Goldin, Stephen, 165

Goss, Leonard G., 59, 146, 179, 223
Graff, Henry F., 170
Greeley, Andrew, 55
Grench, Charles, 158
Griffin, William, 15n
Grooms, Kathe, 145
Guinn, G. Earl, 199
Gunther, Max, 174

Hamilton, Charles, 13
Hanson, Nancy Edmonds, 169
Hanson, Sherman R., 38, 43, 53 64
Hardman, Frank, 134
Hardy, R. Donald, 110
Hardy, Wes, 115
Harrison, H. D., 116
Hastings, Robert J., 167
Hawkins, Robert H., 56, 75
Hawley, Wendell, 70, 155
Hay, Rich, 117
Hayes, J., 111
Hazard, David M., 134
Hearne, Betsy, 165
Heller, Robert T., 65, 136
Hemingway, Ernest, 169
Hendrickson, Stephen J., 140
Herr, Ethel, 169
Hersey, John, 173
Hill, Robert W., 54, 70, 110
Hjelm, Norman, 137
Hoffer, Eric, 73
Hollaway, Ernest L. 212-213, 219n
Honea, Charla H., 155
Hoover, James, 43, 54, 69
Hoskins, Billy O., 152
Howes, Mary Ruth, 110
Hudson, Helen, 155
Hull, Helen, 27, 33n, 173, 174
Hunter, G., 111

Inman, V. Kerry, 129
Irving, John, 68

Jakes, John, 108
Jenkins, Jerry B., 145
Jersey, John, 173
Johnson, Carol A., 131
Johnson, Joe S., 55, 72-73, 132
Johnson, Samuel, 44

Kadushin, Charles, 165
Kammerman, Sylvia E., 165
Karp, Irwin, 89
Kay, D., 142
Kaye, Marilyn, 165
Keith, Bill, 141
Kelsey, Morton T., 111
Keylock, Leslie R., 132
Kidd, H., 171
King, Stephen, 108
Klingbell, Carolyn, 117
Knott, Leonard L., 175
Knott, William C., 166
Kraft, Charles H., 166
Kregel, Robert L., 143
Kuswa, Webster, 171

LaCasce, Steward, 164
Laird, Becky, 138
Lambert, Herbert, 132
Lawler, J. George, 136
Lawson, Penelope, 33n
Leach, Michael, 136
Lee, R. G., 199
LeFever, Marlene, 135
Lehman, Yvonne, 115-116
Levin, B. J., 131
Lewis, C. S., 33n
Loizeaux, Marie, 144
Loudon, John, 138
Luccock, Halford E., 33n, 169, 214
Lunn, M. A., 147

Lynch, Kevin A., 149

MacCampbell, Donald, 174
Mann, Thomas, 173
Marcuse, K., 111
Mark, Dale W., 117
Mark, Joan, 139
Marquardt, Mervin, 135
Mason, Eileen, 139
Mathieu, Aron M., 15n, 166
Maxon, Hazel Carter, 171
May, Rollo, 20-21, 33n
McCarthy, David S., 47n, 171
McClellan, Keith, 110
McConnell, Theodore A., 146
McCormick, Mona, 170
McCullough, David W., 171
McElderry, Margaret K., 42,
    47n
McGinnis, Alan Loy, 111
McGonagle, David, 133
McGraw, Woody, 154
McHale, John J., 134
McKinney, Betty Jo, 129
Meranus, Leonard S., 103n
Meredith, Scott, 175
Meyer, Marion M., 150
Michener, James A., 172, 173
Mikesell, Greg, 137
Millen, Kin, 158
Miller, Arthur, 73
Miller, Henry, 33n
Miller, Mara, 172
Miller, Marge, 154
Montgomery, Herb, 211-212,
    219n
Montgomery, John M., 156
Moore, John A., 172
Morely, Christopher, 32
Morton, H. V., 25
Muir, Virginia, 155
Murray, Donald, 44, 47n
Murry, John Middleton, 33n

Neal, Harry Edward, 30, 33n,
    170
Netteburg, Kermit, 116
New, Bill, 154
Newport, John, 199
Notaro, Thom, 151
Noton, Thomas, 113, 167
Nouwen, Henri, 67
Nutt, Grady, 191
Nygren, Bruce, 57, 75

Oates, Joyce Carol, 108
O'Connell, Raymond T., 151
O'Neill, Eugene, 172
Oveis, Frank, 55, 72

Parker, J. Fred, 116
Pasiciel, Sara, 115
Patterson, Ronald P., 109-110
Paulson, Wayne, 157
Peale, Norman Vincent, 9-10,
    12-13, 16n, 171
Perkins, Max, 170
Perry, Martha, 55-56, 73-74
Peter, Laurence J., 47n
Phillips, Dorothy B., 33n
Pitkin, Ronald E., 148
Plotnik, Arthur, 166
Polking, Kirk, 103n, 164, 173
Porst, Jim, 130
Pott, Jon, 66, 136
Powell, E. A., 164
Powell, Walter, 165
Pradt, Robert W., 150
Priestley, J. B., 24
Pugh, Donald E., 54, 71, 151

Raffclock, David, 47n
Rausenbaum, Veryl, 174
Rawley, Philip, 56-57, 75
Read, Cynthia, 149
Reynolds, Paul R., 170

Reynoldson, Rose, 117
Richards, Frank, *See*
  Charles Hamilton
Richardson, Robert L., 115
Ridenour, Fritz, 152
Rivers, William L., 167, 174
Rockwell, F. A., 168
Roper, Gayle G., 117
Rosenbaum, Jean, 174
Rowell, Edd, 45, 53, 63, 145
Ruark, James E., 38, 53, 67-68
  158

Saunders, Lowell, 115
Schell, Mildred, 172
Schemenaur, P. J., 174
Schrock, Paul M., 140
Seboldt, Roland, 53, 63, 109,
  111, 130
Sehnert, Keith W., 111
Selchen, Frumie, 149
Seward, Sharon, 139
Shatzkin, Leonard, 169
Shedd, Charlie, 169
Sheldon, Sidney, 108
Shepherd, A. "Doc", 16n
Sherer, Michael, 133
Simenon, Georges, 13
Simmons, William T., 135
Simon, Neil, 108
Simpson, Donald, 147
Singer, Megs, 153
Sire, James W., 142, 168
Sky, Kathleen, 165
Sloan, John, 57, 75, 147
Smith, Bailey, 199
Sorensen, Lori J. P., 116
Spangler, Ann, 153
Sparks, Lee, 138
Speiser, Stuart, 103n
Spencer, Sue, 173
Stanley, Hugh, 110

Steen, John Warren, 115
Stobbe, Leslie H., 38, 43, 54
  68-69, 140
Stone, Lawrence M., 148
Streeter, Carole S., 156
Strunk, William, 167
Stuart, Jesse, 171
Sutton, Walt, 143
Talbott, David R., 116
Taylor, Kenneth, 199
Tebbel, John, 170
Teeters, Peggy, 168
Thatcher, Floyd, 123n
Thomas, David St. John, 167
Todd, Alden, 167
Tracy, Wesley, 211, 219n
Trueblood, Elton, 11-13, 16n
  44, 47n
Twain, Mark, 19, 23, 189

Unger, John, 113
Unseth, Nathan, 131

Vajda, Jaroslav J., 135
Van Buren, Abigail, 171
Van Diest, John, 147
Van Gelder, Robert, 173
Van't Kerhoff, Daniel, 53, 65,
  130
Vaughn, Lou (Mrs.), 116
Voltaire, 207

Wales, Tony, 144
Walker, R. W., 171
Wallace, J. O., 150
Ward, Wayne, 199
White, E. B., 167
Whiteside, Thomas, 164
Whitney, Phyllis A., 108
Wickenden, Dan, 47n
Wilke, Jerry A., 128

Wilson, Jill, 145
Wilson, Sloan, 171
Wirt, Sherwood E., x, 5, 15n
    175
Wise, Carroll, 202
Wolf, Virginia, 24
Wolfe, Thomas, 169

Young, Robert D., 33n, 204-205

Zinsser, William, 170